PILOT ERROR

SYLVIA WRIGLEY

Sylvia Wrigley's *Pilot Error*

Looking for a book to keep you grounded? *Pilot Error* is not it. This is not an instructional aviation book, unless you consider it as a crash course in the dangers of taking shortcuts and ignoring common sense. *Pilot Error* is a book about the hilarious, absurd, and sometimes tragic mistakes that pilots can make.

From sex in the cockpit to landing on the wrong runway, this book will keep you flying high with shock and laughter.

PILOT ERROR

2023

UUID# E8F4392D-310B-4291-9951-E7CBC7280CCF

ISBN: 978-9985-4-1380-7

For information address:

sylvia@planecra.sh

EQP BOOKS

The logo consisting of the letters "EQP" over an open book with power cord is a registered trademark of EQP BOOKS.

http://EQPBooks.com/

CONTENTS

Introduction

IN CHOOSING from the many, many incidents and accidents caused solely by the pilot being an idiot, I had to make some choices. I tried to keep a light tone throughout, even when the consequences were serious. This is on the simple principle that if you don't laugh, you'll cry, and a book full of the darkest moments of aviation would be hard for me to write and hard for you to read.

I also chose to focus on modern incidents, by which I mean those from this millennium, by which I mean the past twenty years. But rest assured, that doesn't mean I've forgotten all those older cases; I'm just collecting them separately for a follow-up book!

Drunk and Disorderly

A drunken pilot is a happy pilot but this is maybe not so great for the passengers. It may seem obvious that alcohol and flying don't mix, but some pilots seem to forget this fact. In this section, we'll take a look at the consequences of pilots who fly under the influence, from hilarious radio conversations to dangerous incidents that could have been avoided.

All Boozed Up and Ready To Fly

IT WAS 05:17, just a few minutes past dawn, when the Norwegian police watched the flight crew board the Baltic Air aircraft. The charter flight taking holiday makers from Oslo to the sunny island of Crete was due to depart in half an hour.

There were five crew members: two pilots and three cabin crew. Four of them were drunk.

Whenever something like this comes up, there are always dissenters, often retired pilots, possibly alcoholics, who ask whether the crew were "really" drunk. This Norwegian case was no exception, with the pro–drunk-pilot brigade arguing that maybe the flight crew just had a quick pint before heading off to bed and then were completely unreasonably hauled out of the aircraft by police.

As it happens, the hotel staff and the hotel's CCTV have documented the events of the day and night before the flight, and I think we can all agree that this does not fit the scenario of one quiet beer before bed.

The crew started drinking around four on the Friday afternoon. One of them said later, "We went to the hotel 15 to 16:00 (between 3 and 4 pm) to sit and chat a bit. We were tired, and we must have lost track of how much we drank."

They started on beer, yes. And then they bought two bottles of whisky to share. By 8 pm, both bottles were empty.

After that, it gets a bit hazy. According to the crew, they all stopped drinking at 8 and that was it for the night. However, that doesn't quite mesh with the alcohol levels they demonstrated the morning after.

One of the crew members recalls that she had "some" of the whisky but she wasn't sure how much. She was confident, however, that she'd stopped drinking around eight. Or definitely before nine, anyway. She joined the other crew members in one of the hotel rooms to watch videos but said that she wasn't drinking any alcohol by then.

The timing is legally important. Norwegian law is very clear on this point: airline crews must not have a drink within eight hours of going to work, which meant that legally they should not have consumed any alcohol after 9 pm.

However, even if the airline crew stopped drinking eight or more hours before going to work, they must be below the limit of 0.2 milligrams of ethanol per millilitre of blood. For example, an adult male of average size could drink four pints of beer ten hours before duty and could still fall foul of the law with an alcohol level of .03%.

Most pilots, if they drink at all, are careful not

to drink within twelve hours of going on duty. Truly, most pilots wouldn't even consider having four pints of beer the day before a flight, let alone ten hours before.

When tested, the captain had a blood alcohol level of 0.4, twice the maximum allowed for flight. And his was the lowest blood alcohol level of the crew. The first cabin member tested with blood alcohol levels of 0.55. The second cabin crew member's test showed as 0.91. The first officer's blood alcohol was 1.2 mg.

Translating these numbers into standard responses, the captain would have been suffering from "mild euphoria, decreased inhibitions, diminished attention and judgement", the two cabin crew members with "euphoria, sedation, impaired coordination and decreased judgement" and the first officer with "confusion, disorientation, impaired balance and slurred speech".

Obviously, alcohol tolerance varies by person but, to be honest, at 1.2 mg it is impressive that the first officer was even conscious. In every instance, the crew's alcohol level was too high to legally drive a car, let alone fly a plane.

But once the case came to court, the prosecution was not satisfied to leave it at that. All four crew members stated that they had stopped drinking around 20:00 and certainly before 21:00. In response, the prosecution brought out video footage from the hotel, showing the first officer purchasing beer at the hotel bar. It was 01:39, almost two in the morning, and only a few hours before they were due to arrive at the airport.

The first cabin crew member stuck to her story

that she had not had another drink, although based on the breathalyser, the judge estimated that she must have had a blood alcohol level over 2 when they left the bar in the early evening. "Were you really so drunk?"

She wasn't sure how much she'd had to drink but said that as she'd not eaten and not had any water, she must have metabolised the alcohol more slowly.

The second cabin crew member had a bigger issue to overcome, as she had been spotted in the hotel lobby at two in the morning. She agreed that she was in the lobby but said it was irrelevant, as she definitely didn't drink any alcohol after 21:00. She was very adamant about the time which did nothing to explain the level of alcohol in her bloodstream the following morning. She conceded that she must have been very drunk. "Usually, I do not drink alcohol at all," she said. "I cannot handle alcohol well."

As it happens, she got her timings wrong. By claiming that she hadn't had a drink after 21:00, she was trying to establish that she did not drink anything within eight hours of 5 am. However, according to the airline, her workday started at 04:35. If she stopped drinking at 21:00, she was already 25 minutes too late.

It was twenty to three in the morning when a hotel staff member phoned the police, telling them that an airline crew was drinking at the hotel who were apparently flying that morning.

This doesn't sound like they were all quietly drinking water and watching videos in the hotel room. At the very least, it's clear that they didn't get a wink of sleep before their early morning flight.

Faced with the evidence, the second cabin crew member eventually admitted that yes, she was still in the bar at 03:30, at which point she fell asleep because she was drunk.

It was quarter past five in the morning when the police stopped the crew who were boarding the aircraft and asked them for breathalyser tests. Soon after, the four were arrested. For reference, the full crew for the flight that day was five; only one crew member was sober.

Passengers were told that their flight was cancelled due to illness and to please collect their luggage.

The four crew members were held in custody for two weeks as they were deemed a flight risk.

The first officer was sentenced to six months in prison. The first cabin crew member was sentenced to 45 days, and the second received a 60-day sentence.

The captain was charged with being intoxicated while trying to fly an aircraft, having consumed alcohol less than eight hours before service, and failing to fulfil his responsibilities as captain. He received a ten-month jail sentence.

His defence attorney stated afterwards that the sentencing was too strict, as he had pleaded guilty *only* to being intoxicated while trying to fly an aircraft, which doesn't sound like a great defence. More importantly, he still wasn't accepting responsibility for the flight. As captain, he should have stopped the drunken crew from reporting to work the next morning, not to mention disclosing that he was not fit to fly, let alone command.

It is hard to believe that all four considered it reasonable to drink a few bottles of whiskey the afternoon before a flight, let alone that at least two of them were still drinking after two in the morning. All four were happy to continue the early morning flight with a hundred passengers on board.

The airline issued a press release to say they are introducing additional safety measures: specifically, breathalyser tests for all safety-critical personnel, instead of the random tests previously in force.

It's unlikely that any of the four will ever work in aviation again.

In reading the Norwegian press releases, I used Google Translate to try to get an idea of what the articles said and ended up with this beautiful quote from a passenger of the flight that was cancelled.

> The personnel in the street reported that the crew was ill and unable to fly, and that the flight was cancelled. We therefore went back to the baggage area to retrieve our cases. Then a representative from Air Baltic and gave us matbonger and stated that new crew was on the way. We pretended therefore to be luggage and now waiting for the plane to be set up again, he said.

So now you know: if your flight crew is drunk, simply pretend to be luggage and wait for the next plane.

Highway Patrol Arrest Pilot

On the 15th of July 2022, an officer of the Missouri State Highway Patrol arrested a man for driving while intoxicated on the westbound Interstate 70 at three in the morning.

This is relevant to us because the man was "driving" a single-engine aircraft, a Piper Warrior II. The Piper Warrior was a popular successor to the Cherokee, with longer tapered wings; the Warrior II had improved wheel-fairing aerodynamics and more horsepower.

These improvements did very little to increase its performance on the asphalt concrete of the interstate highway.

The flight was planned from Walker County Airport in Jasper, Alabama to Grain Valley, Missouri, a suburb of Kansas City.

Later, the pilot reported that forty-five gallons of fuel were on board, which, under optimal circumstances, would allow for about five hours of flight in a brand-new aircraft. Usually, a pilot would plan a flight with about an hour's worth of fuel as a buffer. For normal planning, taking into account the fuel used during start-up, taxi and landing, I would estimate that 45 gallons of fuel would allow for about three hours and thirty minutes of flight.

Now, that's a messy back-of-the-matchbook calculation, which does not factor in wind and presumes that the pilot is consistently adjusting the fuel-to-air ratio and not wasting any additional fuel in the climb or by leaving the power setting too high.

Realistically, flying at about 100 knots with a bit of a tailwind, you could *maybe* just about manage 500 nautical miles distance on 45 gallons of fuel if you disregarded the requirement to hold additional fuel in reserve for a diversion or go-around, and if everything went perfectly.

The Piper Warrior II received its airworthiness certificate in 2003, twenty years before the flight. The as-the-crow-flies distance from Walker County Airport to 3GV Airport in Grain Valley is 470 nautical miles.

It was 22:10 when the pilot departed Walker County. It was a dark night but the wind was calm and the visibility was good. He asked air traffic control (ATC) for "VFR Flight Following" service, which meant that the controllers would monitor the flight on radar and offer traffic advisories.

The flight was uneventful until about 40 miles east of Kansas City when the pilot realised that he did not have enough fuel to make it to his destination. He contacted ATC, who responded helpfully with headings to the closest airport for an emergency landing. The pilot did not follow the headings but continued on. The controller then asked the pilot to change to the approach frequency, where he would receive better instructions in order to get him onto the ground safely.

He did not get to the ground safely.

At 02:42, that is, four and a half hours after the pilot had departed Walker County Airport, a highway patrol officer was notified that an aircraft had crash-landed on Interstate 70, completely blocking the westbound lanes.

The officer arrived within ten minutes to see the badly damaged aircraft perpendicular to the roadway with its nose against the guard rail. An ambulance and two police officers from Grain Valley Police Department were already on the scene.

He approached the pilot, who was being treated for his injuries at the ambulance.

The pilot explained that he had departed from Ocala, Florida and that he was en route to Charles B. Wheeler Downtown Airport when he had an emergency.

Ocala, Florida has two airports, Ocala International Airport and Marion County Airport. The pilot had not departed from either of these. He had actually flown from Walker County Airport in Alabama, about 500 miles (800 km) north of Ocala.

"I told the tower I was winchester on fuel," he said.

The highway patrol officer asked him to explain what that meant.

"Winchester on fuel, out of fuel. I ran out of gas."

The Shack Tactical Wiki, a website serving a *ShackTac* veteran gaming community, explains that *winchester* is a military aviation code word to signify that an aircraft is out of ammo.

> A Pilot can declare on the Radio that he is "Winchester" or "Winchester on <ammo/weapon>", letting listeners know that he will not be able to use that weapon until he gets the chance to RTB [return to base] and rearm.

The usage is compared to the term *bingo,* which a military pilot may use to explain that they are out of fuel and need to return to base.

> Pilots may instead decide to stay over the battlefield, knowing they won't be able to make it back to base before the engine sputters out, but hoping to make a difference on the battlefield before they inevitably crash. This is extremely rare in ShackTac.

ShackTac refers to players who take part in multi-player military simulator games.

It's true that the term is legitimately used in military aviation and referenced in the context of US Navy SEALs. This means our unlucky pilot was either an avid military-sim player with a poor attention to detail or a member of an elite special operations force who momentarily got confused as to whether he needed ammunition or fuel to complete his mission to fly home.

It's possible that the controller at the tower understood what the hell the pilot was talking about and that he was out of fuel, not ammunition, but I suspect they also did not have a clue. Certainly, the highway patrol officer didn't.

The pilot kept talking, saying that he was the only occupant of the plane, which, he added, was privately owned and empty. Of both passengers and fuel, although he didn't specify which he meant.

The officer considered that the pilot might be intoxicated. He left him to the emergency services for evaluation while he took a look at the crash site.

An articulated lorry (US: tractor-trailer or semi) was blocking the roadway. It had been heading west to Colorado when the driver noticed the aircraft flying low above her. "He just kept going lower and kept going lower and I'm going WTF. And then the next thing I know, I go holy crap! And he hit the interstate."

The plane came down directly in front of her. Her dashcam footage shows the truck slowing behind the aircraft which was sideways across the fast lane. She stopped her vehicle in the right-hand lane to block the crash site from further traffic. Then she strolled to the wreckage while telling her husband, who was also in the lorry, to call 911. The aircraft rocked and then the pilot's feet came into view as he walked to the tail and then back again. She walked to the far side while her husband stayed in the cab of the lorry and made the phone call.

She offered the officer the dashcam footage

from her lorry and added that she had put the pilot's personal belongings in the cab of her truck. She thought that the police might want them, she said, as the pilot seemed to be a little tipsy.

She handed over a blue backpack and the officer asked her how the pilot had seemed after exiting the aircraft. "Drunk," she said.

She later described him to the local press.[1] "His words were slurring, you could smell the alcohol on him. He gave me a hug and thanked me for blocking traffic and saying that he was glad he didn't hit nobody."

Back at the ambulance, a medic reported that the pilot had requested to be transported for medical care. The medic agreed that the pilot smelled of liquor and was acting intoxicated. However, when asked, the pilot denied consuming alcohol or using drugs and, according to the highway patrol officer, refused any on-site sobriety tests.

The officer decided that, test or no test, the man was drunk. He arrested the pilot at 02:59 on charges of driving while intoxicated and operating an aircraft while intoxicated.

The pilot then volunteered to go with the officer. The officer explained that he was to be transported for medical treatment first, as he had requested.

The pilot said no, he would just go with the highway patrol officer.

The officer asked him for identification and

1   https://www.kshb.com/news/local-news/wit-ness-recalls-moments-leading-up-to-i-70-plane-landing-by-allegedly-intoxicated-pilot

the pilot claimed he did not have any. How, wondered the officer, did he get in and out of airports without any form of identification? The pilot, irritated, said he didn't need ID because they were private airports.

The officer then searched the pilot. In his pocket, the officer found a Kansas State driver's licence and a container of marijuana.

At that point, unprompted, the pilot volunteered new information. "My Glock"—a semi-automatic pistol—"is in the airplane."

The arrest records ended up with a long list of charges: Driving While Under the Influence, Careless and Imprudent Driving Involving a Crash, Felony Possession of a Controlled Substance, Felony Unlawful Possession of a Firearm, Possession of Marijuana (less than 10 grams) and Unlawful Possession of Drug Paraphernalia.

The Piper Warrior II was towed out of the way, and all lanes of the highway were open again by five thirty that morning.

After the accident, the pilot was asked to fill in the NTSB Form 6120.1, a pilot/operator aircraft accident report. Under "Pilot Certificate(s) (Check all that apply)" there is one faint tick mark, under student.

After that, everything is marked N/A (not applicable) or None.

His student pilot certificate was issued in January of 2020. There is not much of an obstacle to getting that certificate if you can pass the medical; however, you should only be flying under the supervision of an instructor, who would obviously never have let him depart on a flight without enough fuel to finish it.

The gentleman—I hesitate to continue calling him a pilot—claimed 290 hours flight time, 235 of which were on this aircraft make and model, which is a particularly high number for a student pilot. For the section titled "Narrative History of Flight," he simply wrote: "Under advisement of council [sic], I decline to answer at this time."

For the form field of "Under Recommendation (How could this accident/incident have been prevented?)" the student pilot shifted to all caps: "DECLINE TO ANSWER UNDER ADVISEMENT OF COUNCIL."

The student pilot claims that he did not refuse the drug and alcohol test on the scene. The Missouri Department of Revenue shows that he'd previously lost his licence for a year for refusing to take a drug or alcohol test. He was also caught driving during that year, this time on a Kansas driver's licence, and a few years later was caught driving on a Nevada licence which had also been suspended. At this point, he probably shouldn't even be issued a fishing licence.

As of writing, the case was still pending. The accused's defence seemed to be based on procedural arguments, specifically that the Missouri State Highway Patrol improperly stopped and arrested him without having a reason to believe that he was flying under the influence. That's an interesting usage of "stopped" as he was definitely on the highway and definitely not going anywhere.

The NTSB have closed their case as the details of the emergency landing are clear.

Law enforcement reported the airplane overflew a tractor-trailer, landed on the interstate roadway, and impacted a guardrail. The airplane sustained substantial damage to the left wing. The student pilot reported to law enforcement that the airplane ran out of fuel. While on-scene at the accident location, the pilot was arrested for driving while intoxicated and operating an aircraft while intoxicated. The pilot refused to provide a statement of the accident.

The National Transportation Safety Board determines the probable cause(s) of this accident to be:

The loss of engine power due to fuel exhaustion.

- Personnel issues: Fuel planning— Pilot
- Aircraft: Fuel—Fluid level
- Personnel issues: Alcohol—Pilot

The role of the NTSB is to evaluate how the accident occurred and what could be done to reduce the chances of such an accident in the future. The answer here seems to be to make sure this man never flies again.

The FAA have confirmed that they are investigating separately.

N28V, I Need Your Call Sign, Please

THIS IS A GENERAL aviation accident that didn't happen on the 27th of April 2017, although it was a near thing.

The aircraft, a 1964 Mooney M20E registration N7828V, was at Rocky Mountain Metropolitan Airport at Broomfield, Colorado. Rocky Mountain Metropolitan Airport is a large airport with an excellent position close to downtown Denver and no airlines. It is extremely popular with general aviation pilots: in 2018 360 aircraft were based there, with 70% of them single engine.

The Mooney is a popular small aircraft although it's known as a "slippery" plane to fly. The variable prop pitch, retractable landing gear and relatively high stall speed mean that the four-seater requires a lot more attention from a pilot than, say, a Cessna 172, which is popular for training.

That morning, the pilot contacted Metro

Tower as he taxied the Mooney out of the hangar. He should have contacted Ground for taxi instructions but the controller took it in his stride.

Mooney: Metro ground, Mooney Seven Eight Two Eight...Victor, ah, coming out of the east T-hangars with information Quebec, umm, current to Three Eight Zero Right.

His aircraft was registered as N7828V. On first contact, one gives the full call sign, where November, for N, is often omitted as it applies to all US-registered aircraft. He's given his location and confirmed that he's listened to the recorded broadcast of the Automatic Terminal Information Service, which offers airport information including what runway is in use. Every time the service is updated, the reference letter increases so that the pilot and the controller can know if they are talking about the same version. Three Eight Zero, however, is a bit of a mystery.

Tower Controller: November 7-8-2-8 Victor, Metro tower. Wind zero eight zero at one zero, which runway would you like?

Mooney: Three eight zero is fine.

Rocky Mountain Metropolitan Airport has three asphalt runways. Two of the runways are parallel.
Runways have up to two digits which signify the compass direction where, for example, a runway heading due south (180°) is referred to as runway 18 and a runway heading due north

is runway 36. (Technically it could be runway 00, although it never is.). Each runway is given two such references, such as 18/36, since the runway in one direction is 180° and the opposite direction is 360°

Parallel runways are assigned L and R to refer to left and right, but obviously which runway is left or right depends on which way you are travelling. The parallel runways at Rocky Mountain Metropolitan have a compass direction of 120° (or 300°). So for the two parallel runways, one of them is 12L/30R and the other one is 12R/30L. That means that if I wanted to fly out on a heading of 120° using the left hand runway (as seen from that direction), I would ask for runway 12 left.

The third runway at Rocky Mountain runs perpendicular to the two parallel runways, from 030° to 210°, so it is referred to as 03/21.

It's pretty easy once you know the logic.

Except that the pilot asked for runway 380. There is no context under which one would refer to a runway with three digits. Even if we accept this as a momentary lapse, it is impossible for there to be a runway 38, as a compass has only 360 degrees.

Tower Controller: November Seven Eight...three eight? We don't have a three eight zero.

It's not clear whether the tower controller fluffed the Mooney's call sign (saying three-eight instead of two-eight) or if his brain just got stuck on the call for 380. Either way, he quickly recovered his professionalism, no doubt assuming the pilot had simply misspoken. It's a rare pilot who has never screwed up a radio call.

Mooney: [Runway] three zero is correct if...if at all possible.

Tower Controller: November 28 Victor, runway three zero right, taxi via Alpha.

The controller has now shortened the call sign, which is his prerogative. Now, the pilot should be using that short form to identify himself. The reason the controller gets to decide how it is shortened is because the controller is the one who knows who else he is talking to and thus can avoid ambiguity. The pilot is cleared to taxi using taxiway Alpha to runway 30R.

Mooney: Taxi via Alpha, three eight zero.

We're back to three eight zero and, again, there's no way to make sense of what this means. It's tagged to the end the way one might confirm a call sign, except that's not his call sign. It isn't a reference to the taxiway, because taxiways are only referred to by letter: they are not assigned numbers to ensure that they don't get confused with runways. It's possible he meant three zero, to refer to the runway, and those pesky eights in his call sign confused him but, if so, he needs to correct this.

Tower Controller: N28V, it's runway three zero *right*. Taxi via Romeo to Alpha.

There are two runway 30s, after all, and it's important he taxi to the correct one. Also, note the more detailed instruction as to how to get to the runway (take taxiway Romeo to get to taxiway Alpha). The controller is starting to get concerned.

Mooney: Romeo to Alpha, uh, Seven Two Eight Victor

When a call sign is abbreviated, a controller generally defaults to using the prefix, in this case November for an N-reg (US) aircraft, plus the last three characters. It's not always that precise in real life, though. When I was flying N666EX, I was referred to by my full call sign (November Six Six Six Echo X-ray) and sometimes a quick version of that (November Triple Six Echo X-ray), and when abbreviated it was sometimes November Six Echo X-ray and sometimes just November Echo X-ray.

The important thing here is that, once a controller has abbreviated your call sign, you can use your full call sign or you can use the same abbreviation. It's common to vary it slightly by using the model in place of the prefix. The pilot did this on the very first call: Mooney Seven Eight Two Eight Victor. In my experience, it is common for pilots not to use either but simply to repeat the final characters of their call sign, for example Two Eight Victor, which they can get away with if it isn't too busy.

Pilot Rudy Jakma tells the story of three Cessna 172s, PH-WVB, PH-HVB and PH-MVB, which were all in Amsterdam's control zone at the same time. This meant that the common shortening of the prefix and last two letters did not work, because they were all Papa Victor Bravo.

The controller, frustrated at the pilots who didn't seem to care that they were all shortening to the same abbreviation, finally sent them all away, snapping, "All aircraft listening to the call sign Papa Victor Bravo, leave my control zone at once, we are too busy."

So, yes, it happens that pilots get used to a specific controller and then continue to shorten their call signs in a common way rather than following the controller's lead. But you *definitely* can't make up your own version of your call sign and expect it to be accepted.

But that's what this guy did. Seven Two Eight Victor is not a sequence that exists in his call sign, N7828V. Although each digit is theoretically there, it's so randomly unidentifiable that he may as well have stuck with 380.

Not to mention the fact that he still hasn't *actually* said which runway he is taxiing to, which should have been part of his callback. The tower controller patiently prompts the pilot with exactly what he needs to say to confirm he knows what he's doing.

Tower Controller: November Seven Eight Two Eight Victor, I need runway three zero right. Runway *three zero right,* taxi via Romeo to Alpha.

Note the controller reverting back to the full call sign here. He may not have done it consciously but it speaks volumes. I think it may have been the ATC equivalent of your mother using your full name when you are in trouble.

The Mooney isn't the only aircraft at the airfield, of course, and there is plenty else that the controller needs to deal with.

At that moment, another plane, a Citation which had just landed, called to say they were exiting the runway. The Mooney's pilot's next transmission was broadcast at the same time which meant that neither was comprehensible. All that could be heard was the pilot very carefully enunciating Two Eight Victor at the end.

Tower Controller: November 28 Victor, you got stepped on. Standby, hold your position please. Citation that just exited, say your call sign.

N339ES: Sorry about that! Three Three Niner Echo Sierra.

The controller dealt with the Citation and turned his attention back to the Mooney.

Tower Controller: November 28 Victor, I need runway three zero right and your call sign, please.

We're not messing around anymore.

Mooney: Three Niner Victor...or Two Eight Victor, uh, taxi via, uh, taa...taxi via alpha... Two Eight Victor.

What? He isn't even close. An aircraft's

registration number is generally on the instrument panel as a small badge, specifically so if you blank out on it, you have it right there in front of you. All he needs to be able to do is read three characters.

Tower Controller: November 28 Victor, runway three zero right and your call sign please, and verify if [you] have information Quebec.

The tower controller already knows his call sign and he knows that the pilot has information Quebec. He's giving the pilot one more chance to correctly read back his clearance to the runway. I suspect he's hoping the pilot will back down and stop trying. But no, the pilot makes one more attempt to respond to the controller.

N7828V: Three eight…Three zero victor and two eight Victor, umm…plat.

OK, maybe he didn't say plat. Maybe he said back. What he didn't say was anything comprehensible.

Tower Controller: November 28 Victor, hold your position, please.

Translation: You are not getting near my runway, buddy.

N7828V: Holding position, Two Eight Victor.

Oh, well done!
In the tower, the controller spoke to a colleague about what was happening. The second controller,

in an inexplicable fit of optimism, recommended that he ask if the pilot had an instructor on board. Maybe he was just a very confused student whose instructor was letting him muddle through?

Tower Controller: November 28 Victor, are you familiar with the airport or have an instructor on board?

N7828V: [heavy sigh] Two Eight Victor is somewhat familiar with the airport, over.

Not good enough.

Tower Controller: November 28 Victor, roger. Hold your position.

N7828V: Holding position, Two Eight Victor.

Both controllers now agreed that there was a problem here. The second controller got on the phone to airport operations and explained the situation. Airport operations called the sheriff's office and then sent staff to speak to the pilot.

Tower Controller: November 28 Victor, uh, go ahead and shut down your engine. Airport wanted to talk to you real quick. They're almost out to you.

N7828V: [another sigh] Two Eight Victor.

At least he got his call sign right.

The pilot taxied back to a hangar and got out to speak to the airport officers. When the sheriff arrived he immediately noted that the pilot's eyes were red and watery and he was having difficulty standing, even though he apparently thought he was competent to fly. When he spoke, his speech was slurred and there was no missing the smell of alcohol on his breath.

The sheriff attempted a field sobriety test. The pilot could not quite understand the text. Finally, the sheriff gave up and arrested him.

Back at the station, the pilot completed a breathalyser test which gave a result of a .207 BAC or the equivalent of 200mg per 100ml ethanol in his blood.

The federal blood alcohol limit for pilots is .04 BAC. The FAA further prohibits drinking any alcohol within eight hours of flying.

The controllers won an Archie League Award for their quick actions in this case. You can hear the actual ATC on YouTube by searching for Archie League Awards Northwest Mountain Region Winning Flight Assist: Bancroft & Mailloux.[2]

The airport terminated the hangar lease for the Mooney immediately. The Mooney was subsequently sold to a new private owner, who had nothing to do with this crash-that-didn't-happen. That same aircraft almost crashed in 2011, when the controls jammed as the aircraft was landing at a Florida airport. It turned out that a small flashlight had fallen through the interior cockpit boot and into the controls. The owner of the flashlight has never been found.

That Mooney is lucky to be alive, that's all I can say.

---

2   https://www.youtube.com/watch?v=7KGWM-00p7Rg

Aircraft Parked at the Pub

SOMETIMES AN AVIATION incident makes the news just for the amazing headline potential, like this incident in 2014.

Man in Australia Arrested for Driving Wingless Plane to Bar

Plane Taxied Down Main Street to Newman Pub

Fine for Man Who Taxied Plane Down Newman Street and Stopped at Pub

The original incident, which took place in 2014, does not disappoint.

A 37-year-old Australian purchased a single-engine two-seater aircraft, a Beechcraft Skipper. The Skipper was designed by Beechcraft as a low-cost training aircraft to compete with the Cessna 150. Unfortunately, it was introduced in 1979 and the US was on the cusp of yet another recession. That year, the second energy crisis of the decade contributed to gas prices increasing by over 50% and homeownership costs went through the roof. In 1979, the inflation rate was 11.35%. To put this into perspective, the US inflation rate was 1.23% in 2020 and, in 2022, 6.5% Effectively, it was bad luck: general belt-tightening meant that less money was being spent in aviation and the demand for new training aircraft was nothing like enough to support the production costs, let alone what Beechcraft invested into design. The result was that just 47 aircraft were produced that year, with a further 140 in 1980 and 125 in 1981 before they stopped production completely. 312 aircraft were produced, most of which went to Beech Aero Centers' flight school network.

The Skipper's wings use a design based on 1970s NASA research to allow for safer low-speed flying. This model, purchased by the Australian gentleman, was not as aerodynamic as the original, however, as it did not have wings.

It isn't clear why he bought the Skipper but after the purchase, he climbed into the cockpit and taxied it away. Small aircraft have steerable nose wheels which are controlled with the rudder pedals. To turn right, you push the right pedal forward and to go left, you press the left pedal. The control column does nothing and, in training, students are often told to put their hands on their lap to keep them from instinctively trying to steer with it.

He was travelling through the Western Australian town of Newman, a modern mining town. I guess he planned to taxi the aircraft to his home, on the opposite side of town. However, on the way home, a great thirst (and possibly the desire to show off his new purchase) overwhelmed him, so he stopped at the Newman Hotel to have a drink at the hotel bar, The Purple Pub.

Aircraft parked at the pub

A police photograph shows the Skipper neatly parked between the lines with two traffic cones put at the front on either side of the propeller. Next to it is a police car which is not, it must be said, quite so expertly parked.

The driver of the aircraft—he was not a pilot—was found in the pub. The locals of Newman, described as "an outback mining town", had greeted him with laughs and praise but the Newman police were less impressed, describing the man as "pretty stupid" and stating that he will face charges "if an appropriate offence can be found."

It is quite clear from the news article that the policemen attending the scene were out of their depth. "It could have been very ugly. All he needed was one gust of wind...because without the wings, it's not very stable...it was a pretty stupid thing to do."

They started with a breath test for alcohol, which he passed. He did not cause any traffic incidents while on the road. He did not attempt to avoid arrest.

"I'm confident that he will be charged with something soon," the local police sergeant said.

Local news, also unclear on the basics of aviation, reported that the aircraft travelled down the street with its propeller running and was, shock horror, being steered by foot pedals. The policeman also said that the fact that the plane did not have a steering wheel made the situation very dangerous.

The only authority with the actual aviation knowledge to deal with the case would be the Australian Civil Aviation Safety Authority (CASA), but as the vehicle had no wings and the driver didn't have a pilot's licence, this case was not actually within their remit. What were they going to do, ban him from flying with his aircraft which had no wings?

That said, there are enough injuries caused by propellers on airfields, let alone one running on the open road and starting up in a pub parking lot.

The Beechcraft Skipper has a capacity of 30 gallons of fuel split between the fuel tanks in each wing. The fuel is fed from the wings through a valve in the centre floorboard to the engine-driven fuel pump. Obviously a workaround was needed, and the Australian gentleman rigged up a system by placing a jerry can full of fuel in the rear of the cockpit, with a tubing running along the outside of the aircraft to the engine.

The police had finally found something to charge the pilot with. They accused him of leaving the engine in a potentially dangerous condition with the ignition on, citing a charge of "Endangering Life, Health or Safety of a Person".

In the end, the prosecution focused on the issue of the propeller running as it ~~taxied~~ drove down busy streets with many pedestrians. The owner of the aircraft pleaded guilty and was fined $5,000 plus court and towage costs. I suppose at least they saved him having to push it back across the parking lot in order to get back onto the road.

He told the press that he was keen to restore the Beechcraft once it was returned to him by police but, no, he wasn't planning on further excursions across the mining town. "I don't think I'll be taking it to the pub again, no."

The police managed to get a better spokesman by the end of the debacle, who at least acknowledged that the story had a lighter side. "The concern is, it did present a real danger to other motorists and pedestrians in what is quite a busy town. The obvious message is, don't drive your plane down the street."

And if you do, maybe go straight home. If he hadn't stopped at The Purple Pub, he might have gotten away with it.

A friend of the aircraft owner spoke out in his defence. "I have indulged in quite a few beverages with this incredible man and am proud as punch to say he is my friend. He is a character and has on several occasions made me laugh so hard I suffered from extreme soreness in the belly regions. He is extremely intelligent and lives the dream with his lovely wife and children, although I wonder how long his wife's sanity will last."

It does seem like being married to this person would be quite a trial in itself!

The Lost Pilot

Have you ever been lost? It's a frustrating experience, especially when you're on a tight schedule. Now imagine being lost in the air, with hundreds of passengers depending on you to land safely. In this section, we'll explore the hilarious and sometimes deadly consequences of pilots who haven't the foggiest idea where they are.

That Airport Must Be Here Somewhere

T HE CAPTAIN WAS KNOWN among his colleagues as a defensive man. First officers who had flown with him complained that he didn't integrate them into his operating procedures or include them into the decision-making process. One reported that he had become lost during a sight-seeing trip in the Alps with thirty passengers on board. They were flying to Sion Airport in Switzerland and he realised that they should have seen it by now. He spotted the airfield and immediately started descending.

The problem was, he had not seen Sion at all. He was descending towards Aosta aerodrome, which was 50km to the south and in Italy. During the approach, there was no discussion and the captain ran through the checklists from memory in a random order. The first officer tried repeatedly to contact Sion aerodrome control but could not get through, as terrain was in the way. The captain failed to react to the first officer's concerns and continued on, making descending turns towards the wrong airport without radio contact.

On the final approach, the passengers looked out the windows to see road signs in Italian. It was only then that the captain realised that he was approaching the wrong airport and initiated a go-around. He flew over St Bernhard's pass into the Rhone valley, where they landed safely in Sion.

As there was no incident, the situation was not reported. If it had been, perhaps the tragic story that I'm about to tell you could have been avoided.

It was a Friday, the 23rd of November 2001. The captain started his flying day at a Swiss flight academy where he worked as an instructor. He met a student pilot at Zurich airport for a training flight. Afterwards, he flew four scheduled flights for the airline, passenger flights between Tirana and Milan-Malpensa. He left Zurich after a total of 15 hours and 31 minutes flight duty time and arrived home about thirty minutes later.

That same day, the first officer also flew four scheduled flights but on a different route: round trips between Budapest and Dusseldorf. He left Zurich with a flight duty time of 10 hours and 15 minutes and commented to his spouse that night that his working day had been very stressful and that he felt exhausted.

The following day, Saturday the 24th of November, the captain started his day at the flying school at 07:30, after a rest time of about 11 hours. He flew multiple instrument training flights with a student who said that they finished the debriefing at 13:30.

The first officer's flying day started at 16:20 after 18 hours rest.

Their first flight together was from Zurich to Berlin Tegel in a British Aerospace AVRO 146-RJ100, owned and operated by the airline.

The flight was delayed and arrived in Berlin at 19:25, forty minutes after the scheduled time of arrival. The flight crew agreed that they did not need to refuel and the passenger catering was already on board. Thus, the flight just needed to be cleaned and checked ready for the return flight. A group of twenty-one passengers did not show up out of the 49 expected, so they loaded the twenty-eight passengers and 23 pieces of luggage.

Flight 3597 departed Berlin-Tegel airport on time for the scheduled flight to Zurich. The captain was the Pilot Flying and the first officer was the Pilot Monitoring, which meant that he was responsible for radio communications and for watching over the different aspects of the flight in order to support the Pilot Flying.

The captain asked the first officer to interpret the runway report and then lectured him at length on the subject, despite the fact that the first officer had actually deciphered the report competently and more or less completely.

That first officer was not a good match for the domineering captain. His personnel records showed that although he was well-qualified and had a good skill level, four different recruitment officers all made comments along the lines that he had "a tendency to subordinate himself". He was described as lively but not aggressive and his assessments noted that he needed to develop self-confidence and personal maturity.

Thus, he did not argue when the captain, with forty times more flying experience than the first officer, treated the first officer as a student rather than as a partner in the cockpit.

Other than that, the flight departure and cruise were uneventful.

Air Traffic Control cleared the flight to descend to FL240 (24,000 feet) for their approach to Zurich. The captain gave an approach briefing and said that he expected an instrument approach on the ILS (Instrument Landing System) to runway 14.

The first officer interrupted to draw the captain's attention to their speed which was "going into the red". The captain reduced speed and told the first officer that he should handle the navigation set up: "Then, er, the NAV setting is up to you."

The captain's personnel reports also showed some disturbing trends, including that he often didn't follow procedure and didn't use his checklists effectively. He'd struggled with an earlier conversion course for the McDonnell Douglas MD-80, with a note in his file saying "it became apparent that [the captain] was having major problems with the MD-80's digital guidance system".

According to his file, he was defensive in relation to more complex technical systems and "frequently exhibited difficulty with their operation".

Despite this, no one undertook any additional performance checks or examinations as to the reasons for his repeated failures.

The first officer changed frequency to Zurich Arrival East Sector and reported that they'd received the recorded airport information referenced as KILO. This automated information service gives airport information and every time it is updated, a new identifier is attached in alphabetical order. The flight crew had listened to the recorded information KILO but since then it had been updated twice, to LIMA and then to MIKE. Information KILO confirmed the Captain's prediction of an instrument approach to runway 14. The newer information warned of worsening weather and to expect a VOR/DME approach to runway 28.

The controller didn't comment that they were out of date with the recording that they listened to but did tell them that the runway had changed.

The flight crew were expecting a precision approach to Runway 14 which involves following a pre-defined glide slope defined by the radio-navigation signals of the Instrument Landing System (ILS).

Runway 28 doesn't have an ILS so now they had to plan a new and more complicated approach.

The captain responded in the cockpit with, "Oh shit, that as well? Fine, OK."

The recorded airport information received another update to NOVEMBER with new weather information: broken clouds were forming at 1,500 feet above the airfield. Again, the controller didn't think to notify the flight crew that the information had been updated since they listened. The flight crew had no reason to realise that their weather information was out of date.

The captain gave a new approach briefing, this time for the standard VOR/DME approach for runway 28.

A VOR/DME approach is a non-precision approach. Rather than simply following a glide slope, you need to track a specific radial towards or away from a VOR station. After you pass the final approach fix, you reduce your altitude at specific intervals (called step downs) which are defined for each runway approach. As you approach the airfield, you should have the runway (and surrounding terrain) in sight and be able to finish your approach visually.

Throughout this, the VOR gives you positional guidance, that is, you are tracking your position laterally using the VOR. The DME tells you your distance from the runway. The step downs are staggered descents based on your DME distance, which ensures that you remain safely above the terrain and obstacles as you approach the runway.

As you calibrate your height to your distance, you continue your descent to the *minimum decision altitude* for the non-precision approach. Once you reach this altitude, you *must* stop your descent unless you have the runway in sight and can continue the landing visually. You can continue your approach at (but not below) the minimum decision altitude until you reach the *missed approach point,* which is a specific distance, by DME, from the runway. If you cannot see the runway once you have reached the missed approach point, you *must* break off the approach and climb away.

At Zurich, Runways 14 and 16 are equipped with a minimum safe altitude warning system (MSAW).

This triggers a visual and acoustic warning in the control tower if an aircraft goes lower than the predefined minimum altitudes. Runway 28 is not equipped with this safety system.

Zurich Arrival cleared the flight for the VOR/DME approach to runway 28 and instructed the crew to reduce speed to 180 knots before asking them to contact Zurich Tower.

Normally, there would be four air traffic controllers working the control tower. However, on this day, the crew was reduced to two staff, and the supervisor had left the tower.

The aircraft descended through 5,000 feet above mean sea level and turned right to fly the final approach at about 11 nautical miles east of Zurich. During the right turn, the captain told the first officer that he had visual ground contact.

The minimum descent altitude is 2,400 feet.

The flight ahead of them was the first to execute the changed approach into runway 28 that evening. That flight crew reported to Zurich Tower that the weather was uncomfortably close to the minimums, by which they meant that they were not able to see the runway until the last minute.

This was important information for the other aircraft arriving, who needed to know that visibility was so poor that they might not be able to land under the current circumstances. The weather was worse than had been reported on the recorded airport information and, quite frankly, does not appear to be good enough for non-precision approaches into runway 28.

Flight 3597 was next in line. The flight descended to 4,000 feet above mean sea level, travelling at 160 knots with a descent rate of about 1,000 feet per minute, which shortly thereafter increased to 1,200 feet per minute. This is an accelerated descent, probably meant to attempt to beat the weather. It was not in line with the step downs: the flight was deviating from the approach path it was meant to be taking.

Despite this, the first officer reported to tower that they were established on final approach.

The flight crew completed the final checks.

The air traffic controller noticed on the runway that the aircraft was low, at just 3,600 feet above mean sea level even though it was still six nautical miles away from the airport. The flight was not following the step-downs and clearly not "established", which is to be stable and following the minimum crossing altitudes. However, as the aircraft was under its own navigation, the controller did not try to correct the flight crew and did not monitor the aircraft's altitude.

In the cockpit, the captain claimed he had visual ground contact.

At that altitude, in the clouds, in that visibility, it is not possible that the captain could have seen the airfield. At best, he was catching glimpses of the hilly terrain that they were flying over.

The first officer, as Pilot Monitoring, is meant to call out when the approach lights or runway are clearly in sight. Nothing was in sight. The first officer should have argued that they did not have sufficient visual reference but he didn't. He simply said, "Yes."

They continued the descent.

"Someone said he saw the runway late

here," said the captain, clearly referring to the previous flight. "Approaching minimum descent altitude...here, we've got some ground contact."

The aircraft descended straight through the minimum descent altitude at 2,400 feet.

"two four (2,400), the minimum. I have ground contact. We're continuing at the moment. It appears we have ground contact, we're continuing on."

The first officer quietly repeated "Two four" under his breath.

What, exactly, could they see?

These images were created with a simulator as a part of the investigation, looking at conditions similar to the incoming flight.

Runway 28 as seen from the VDP at 2,390 feet with a visibility of more than 10km

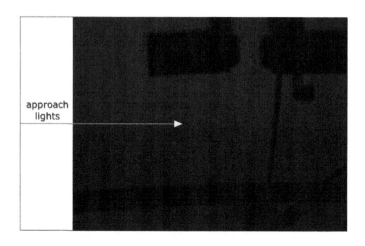

approach
lights

Runway 28 as above with a visibility of 5km

On that cloudy night, the flight crew had visibility of about two kilometres, less than half of the image above. The approach lights at this distance can be detected at the *earliest* at 2.3 nautical miles. The flight coming in before them said on the radio that they were able to see the runway when they were 2.2 nautical miles from the threshold.

If the captain were to attempt a final approach from the minimum descent altitude at this distance, he would need to descend at an angle of 6° towards the runway threshold, too steep for a stabilised approach.

The aircraft was 4.8 nautical miles away from the runway threshold when they descended below the minimum descent altitude.

There's no way they could have seen anything. It was impossible that the commander could see the approach lights and the runway in the distance. They were literally flying blind.

It is the Pilot Monitoring's job to call when the approach lights or runway are clearly in sight. It is the Pilot Monitoring's responsibility to call attention to deviations from procedure and watch both for the decision height and the minimum descent altitude.

The first officer, in his supporting role as Pilot Monitoring, remained silent.

At least the equipment was doing its job: the Ground Proximity Warning System announced that they were just 500 feet above the ground. The flat land here is at 1,500 feet above sea level, with hills rising to 2,000 feet. The aircraft was below the minimum descent altitude and still descending.

Instead of breaking off the approach, the commander reacted with frustration. "Shit, two miles, he said, he saw the runway."

Again, he was referring to the previous flight inbound to Zurich who stated that the weather for runway 28 was "pretty minimum" and that they had the runway in sight at about 2.2 nautical miles away.

But flight 3597 wasn't two miles out. They were still four miles out and descending fast. The captain's frustration showed that he knew that he didn't have the runway in sight, despite deliberately continuing past the minimum descent altitude.

He called out that they were at 2,000 feet but did not seem to notice their DME distance which told him exactly how far they were from the runway. He was likely completely focused on looking out the window, searching for the lights. He made no further mention of having the runway—or anything—in sight. Over the hilly slope, low banks of cloud were forming between 1,800 and 2,000 feet.

The Ground Proximity Warning System sounded an alert: MINIMUMS, MINIMUMS. They were just 300 feet above the ground. At the same time, the Tower controller, who had equally not noticed that they were still miles away and low, cleared the flight to land.

A timid statement from the First Officer: "do a go around?"

At that moment, they still could have saved themselves. If the first officer had initiated a go-around at that moment, as is within his role in an unstabilised approach with no sign of the runway, he would have saved the flight. Instead, he asked hesitantly whether they should.

Within seconds, the captain called for a go around and switched off the auto-pilot. They were so close to the ground, it was possible that he saw the trees in the landing lights.

The first officer called out "Go around!" The power levers were pushed towards the take-off thrust position and the engines RPM started to increase.

It was already too late.

One second later, the Cockpit Voice Recorder recorded the sounds of the aircraft smashing into the trees. It burst into flames as it travelled another 50 metres and crashed into the ground. The recording stopped.

A survivor who was seated in 14B described the scene: "suddenly a loud crashing noise could be heard and the aircraft shook violently.

I immediately looked forward and saw through the open cockpit door and the cockpit windscreens that outside the aircraft a real shower of sparks was rising. Next moment there was a massive impact..."

It took the Zurich airport fire brigade six minutes to arrive at the location.

White-yellow flames burned and there were several small explosions.

Twenty-one passengers and three crew members died at the site of the accident. Seven passengers and two cabin crew members survived. The impact and immediate fire destroyed the cockpit, the front part of the fuselage, the central part of the fuselage and large sections of both wings.

Another first officer came forward after the accident and said that he had flown with the captain a few years earlier, for an approach to Lugano at night in instrument conditions. The captain, as Pilot Flying, had configured the aircraft for landing early and then selected a rate of descent for 4,000 feet per minute. The first officer queried this, as the standard rate of descent for that approach was 2,000 feet per minute but the captain told him that the procedure could be implemented in this way. At 300 feet above the ground, he broke off the descent and flew along the lake shore and the mountainside until the runway came into view and he was able to land.

The captain clearly believed that it was reasonable to descend below the minimum descent height, even at night and in instrument conditions. His records showed that he struggled with digital navigation aids and complex technical systems. He did not work with his co-pilots as a team but instead simply reinforced his position of authority.

Over time, we have learned that the interaction in the cockpit is vital to the safe management of critical phases of flight. The Pilot Monitoring, often the less experienced first pilot, must be confident enough to speak up and the Pilot Flying must be willing to accept his support.

But in this case, both pilots had exhibited problematic behaviour, behaviour logged as a part of their training and their personnel files, that showed they were not exhibiting the high levels of competence required of a commercial pilot.

The combination of both those pilots in the cockpit of flight 3597 was fatal: a complicated approach in minimum conditions flown by an authoritarian commander paired with a first officer who didn't have the strength to argue.

The decision to continue the descent into foggy ground was possibly affected by the commander's fatigue as well as his lack of technical prowess. He appears to have hoped desperately to make visual contact rather than to reference his instruments.

Throughout the dangerous final approach, the first officer said nothing and took no recorded actions, from the time when the aircraft descended past the minimum descent altitude to his final hesitant question of whether they should go around. It appears that he recognised their descent without visual references as an error and yet did not have the confidence to take action.

Um, Have You Landed?

Flight SWA4013 was a Southwest Airlines scheduled passenger service from Chicago, Illinois to Branson, Missouri on the 14th of January, 2014.

In the cockpit was

- the captain, who was Pilot Monitoring,
- the first officer, who was Pilot Flying,
- a company dispatcher who was observing from the flight deck jumpseat.

The Boeing 737-700 departed late that evening. As they climbed away from Chicago, the flight crew discussed their destination. The captain had never flown into Branson Airport before and the first officer had only been to the airfield once, using runway 32.

Based on the wind conditions that night, they agreed that runway 14 would be in use for landing. Runway 14 didn't have an Instrument

Landing System (ILS), so they planned to fly a visual approach backed up by an RNAV (area navigation) instrument approach.

Usually, a flight will either use a visual approach or an instrument approach. This evening, they planned to do a combination.

The Pilot Flying would fly the approach while keeping visual with the runway and at the same time, the Pilot Monitoring would track the navigation beacons in order to ensure that they remained on course. His navigation display would show him the aircraft position, the distance and bearing to the navigation beacon, and the ground speed or time to the navigation beacon.

The captain set up the distance measuring equipment (DME) for the localiser on runway 32, a navigational beacon located on the far end of the runway. This should have made it trivial to navigate to the right place.

The sun set while they were flying, at about a quarter past 5. About ten minutes later, the first officer, in his role as Pilot Flying, began a standard briefing for the Branson Airport approach. He expected air traffic control to give him radar vectors to lead him to the approach, and then he would use the captain's RNAV to line them up with the runway for a visual final approach and landing. He confirmed the important numbers: the final approach course was 143° and the elevation at the touchdown point was 1,278 feet above mean sea level.

The Boeing 737-700 requires 4,700 feet (1,432 metres). This was fine as the runway at Branson was 7,140 feet long (2,176 metres).

Next, the first officer and the captain discussed what they would do after landing to taxi to the gate. The first officer initially thought that they could turn directly off the runway onto the taxiway back to the gate. After some discussion, they decided that for runway 14, they would need to make a 180° turn and head back in order to exit to the taxiway.

Springfield Air Traffic Control (ATC) cleared the flight to descend to 24,000 feet and then, a few minutes later, cleared them direct to Branson Airport. The crew picked up the automated weather report and airport information, which confirmed that runway 14 was in use. As the aircraft descended through 18,000 feet, the first officer called for the descent checklist.

They were about 60 nautical miles (110 km) northeast of Branson Airport when the controller cleared the flight to descend to 4,000 feet and to expect a visual approach to runway 14. The controller told them to proceed directly to the VUCUG waypoint, which is the final approach fix for the RNAV runway 14 approach.

Everything was happening exactly as planned. There was a conversation in the cockpit that they would put a 5- and 10-mile ring around "it", presumably referring to Branson Airport's location on their navigation display.

All three crew discussed their route and current location. They compared the navigation fixes and stations on their navigation display to the city lights that they could see out of the window. They all agreed which lights were Branson and which lights were Springfield, by which they probably meant the lights of Springfield-Branson National Airport, another airport which was around 50 miles (80 km) to the northwest.

As Branson Airport does not have the ability to monitor aircraft on radar, Springfield ATC provided the approach services. The controller contacted Branson Airport Tower to say that the flight SWA4013 was currently 20 miles northeast of Branson Airport for a visual approach to runway 14.

They weren't *quite* visual yet. The first officer said, "Well, I see the beacon down there... No runway yet."

The captain responded, "I think that's it. I see a bunch of bright white lights to the right and just a little to the left of the beacon."

At this point, Springfield ATC interrupted their conversation to advise that the runway was located at their eleven o'clock and one five (15) miles. That is to say, the airport was 15 miles out and slightly to the left, where twelve o'clock would be straight ahead.

Now, the controller was a bit slapdash. He said 15 miles but actually, Branson Airport was almost twenty miles out and really, it was at their ten o'clock position.

The crew looked out and compared visual references and then the captain responded to Springfield ATC to say that they had the airfield in sight.

At 18:03, Southwest flight 4013 was cleared for a visual approach to runway 14. Springfield ATC terminated their radar service and advised the crew to contact Branson Airport Tower, who were expecting their call.

The flight crew configured the Boeing 737 for landing and completed their landing checklist. They exchanged callouts tracking their speed, altitude, glide path and sink rate until they crossed the threshold of the runway.

The aircraft touched down at 300 feet past the displaced threshold.

Unfortunately, they were not on runway 14 at Branson Airport, with a roomy 7,140 feet (2,176 metres) for them to come to a halt.

Instead, they were on runway 12 at M. Graham Clark Downtown Airport (PLK), about seven miles north of Branson Airport.

The runway here was just 3,738 feet (1,140 metres), almost half the length that they were expecting.

The dry runway landing distance for the Boeing 737 using maximum manual braking and reverse thrust is 2,820 feet, but of course, that's presuming you are expecting to make a short landing.

In between the callouts for the speedbrake, thrust reversers and the autobrakes, the captain said, "This ain't it."

He immediately applied maximum braking. The Boeing 737 came to a stop about 300 feet from the end of the paved surface of runway 12.

Once they had come to a complete halt, the captain contacted Branson Airport Tower.

"Tower, [this is] Southwest 4013."

"Southwest 4013, go ahead."

The captain took a deep breath and then came

out with it. "Ah. I assume I'm not at your airport."

A long pause followed.

The Branson Tower controller eventually spoke. "Southwest 4013..." Another pause. "Ummm, have you landed?"

"Yeah."

Another pause. "Southwest 4013, roger."

I guess there's not a lot more you can say.

M. Graham Clark Downtown Airport, located just outside of the village of Point Lookout, Missouri, is a small general aviation airport which services single and multi-engine planes and helicopters. It does not have air traffic control. Airfield lighting is activated by a pilot-controlled lighting system. If the flight crew had been a little bit luckier, the lights would have been off and they would never even have known that the airport was there.

The controller at Branson Airport tower said that to save money, he normally kept the runway edge lights off until the aircraft was reported on arrival. There's no log to show when the runway lights were turned on that night, but the controller believes that he turned them on at 18:00, when he was notified by Springfield ATC that the flight was inbound. Before the lights were turned on, only the runway end identifier lights and the precision approach slope indicator could help the crew locate the airfield.

It was about 1800 when the flight crew were looking out at the city lights and trying to identify the airport. They were cleared for a visual approach at 18:03.

When the Springfield controller advised the

crew that the runway was located at eleven o'clock and 15 miles out, he inadvertently led them to look almost directly at the Downtown Airport. Branson Airport was slightly to the left: at their ten o'clock position and almost twenty miles out.

The flight crew noticed that they were a little high on the approach and so they widened the base leg. As far as the controller was concerned, it looked like they were on the right flight path into Branson until radar was lost, which was normal for when aircraft on approach to Branson descended below 2,600 feet.

Once the pilots had the runway in sight, they did not reference any of the on-board navigation. Thus, they never realised that they were six miles out and twenty degrees off.

This was the responsibility of the Pilot Monitoring. The first officer, as Pilot Flying, needed to be looking out at the runway and concentrating on his visual approach. But the captain should have been monitoring the navigation instruments as a crosscheck. He had set up the DME from the runway 32 localizer, the beacon at the end of the runway they were meant to be going to, specifically so that he could confirm their location in the final approach. But instead of monitoring the navigational instruments, the captain used the heads-up display in VMC (Visual Meteorological Conditions) mode, which allowed him to monitor their rate of descent. This mode does not provide any navigational assistance or flight director guidance.

And so, there they were.

The Branson Tower controller contacted

Springfield ATC.

"Did you watch Southwest land?"

"Yeah, why?"

"Did you see him come here?"

"Say that again?"

"He said he landed at the wrong airport."

"Are you kidding?"

"No, I'm not."

"He dropped off (radar) about over Point Lookout."

"I think that's where he landed. I'll call you back."

He was right. The airline sent out a couple of busses with a few baggage handlers and ground crew to Point Lookout to pick up the passengers and their bags. As luck would have it, a set of airstairs was available at the smaller airport, so the passengers did not have to slide down the wings.

It's an awfully short runway for a 737 but a crew was brought in to fly it out of Point Lookout, empty and without refuelling.

The captain and first officer were removed from flying duties immediately and suspended with full pay pending an internal investigation. The captain has now returned to his flying duties. The first officer elected to retire.

Giant 4241 Heavy, Confirm You Know Which Airport You Are At

THE BOEING 747 DREAMLIFTER is a specially modified jet designed to haul large cargo. It's big, with a wing span of 211 feet, which means that balanced on its side it would be taller than the Cinderella Castle; and, at 235 feet long, it's longer than the height of a Giant Sequoia. The modified 747 can carry cargo up to 87,346 pounds, with a maximum total weight of 800,000 pounds.

The interior looks like the inside of a hangar and it is routinely used to transport assembly pieces for the Boeing 787 Dreamliner to Boeing's final assembly site. It needs just over 9,000 feet of runway to take off when fully laden, about 2,800 metres. This was unfortunate for the 747 Dreamlifter operated by Atlas Air when it found itself at Jabara Airport with a runway that was just 6,101 feet long.

The Dreamlifter was meant to be picking up

B-787 fuselage parts at McConnell Air Force Base in Wichita, Kansas that evening for delivery to Boeing in Seattle, Washington.

The aircraft departed New York's John F. Kennedy International Airport at 19:26 local time, bound for McConnell AFB. The flight was without incident and, as far as the crew were concerned, everything was looking good. They were in contact with the tower frequency of McConnell Air Force Base and reported that they were inbound for runway 19L using the RNAV (GPS) approach. This is a method of navigation (aRea NAVigation) which uses inertial navigation in the aircraft in conjunction with ground-based beacons and GPS in order to establish its position and groundspeed. You'd think, under the circumstances, that it would be relatively clear which airport you were flying into.

The Dreamlifter's call sign is Giant 4241 heavy.

Giant 4241 heavy: Good evening, McConnell Tower. Giant 4241 heavy is on the...er, GPS, RNAV GPS approach 19 left.

McConnell Tower: Giant 4241 heavy, McConnell Tower. Check wheels down. Runway 19 left, wind 140 at 4, cleared to land.

Giant 4241 heavy: Clear to land, runway 19 left, wheels down. Giant 4241 heavy.

McConnell Tower: Giant 4241 heavy, check wheels down.

Giant 4241 heavy: Giant 4241, go ahead.

McConnell Tower: Giant 4241 heavy, check wheels

down and expect a mid-field turnoff at Delta.

Now these are all normal calls for a normal approach. McConnell Air Force Base (KIAB) is four miles south of Wichita, with a control tower and two runways of 12,000 feet which run parallel to each other. It also has an ALSF1 approach lighting system with strobe lights on the approach path.

The Dreamlifter is cleared to land on the left-hand runway with instructions as to where to exit the runway to the taxiway. Everything should be straightforward.

The next call, however, makes it clear that something isn't right.

Giant 4241 heavy: Giant 1440...4241. We might. We'll get back to you here momentarily, we're not on your approach.

McConnell Tower: Giant 4241 heavy, McConnell is 9 miles south of you.

Giant 4241 heavy: Uh, yes sir. We just landed at the other airport.

Colonel James Jabara Airport is nine miles northeast of Wichita handles small planes: general aviation and air taxi traffic. It has a single concrete runway 18/36, which is half the length of the parallel runways at the air force base. It does not have a control tower.

Giant 4241 heavy: Uh, apparently we've landed at BEC.

McConnell Tower: Giant 4241 heavy, verify you're on the ground at Beech Airport?

Giant 4241 heavy: We think so.

BEC is Beechcraft Factory Airport, which lies between Jabara and McConnell. They aren't at Beech Airport at all, but they don't know that yet.

McConnell Tower: Giant 4241 heavy, McConnell Supervisor. Verify you are full stopped and landed. Stopped at BEC airport?

Giant 4241 heavy: Affirmative

McConnell Tower: Giant 4241 heavy, McConnell Tower. Are you able to make an approach, uh, a departure off that airport and back in the air to McConnell?

Giant 4241 heavy: Tower, we're working on those details now sir.

McConnell Tower: Roger.

About four minutes pass before they speak up again.

Giant 4241 heavy: And McConnell Tower, Giant 4241.

McConnell Tower: Giant 4241 heavy, McConnell Tower.

Giant 4241 heavy: Yes sir, do you have a quick, is there a tower frequency here? For Beech?

McConnell Tower: Giant 4241 heavy, Beech Tower is actually closed at this time.

Giant 4241 heavy: Okay. Is there a Unicom frequency?

Unicom frequencies are used at airfields where there's no active control tower. They may be staffed by ground personnel who can offer advice. Local aircraft can also use the frequency to announce what they are doing, effectively keeping in contact with all other aircraft traffic in the local area. As the 747 is blocking the runway, it's important that they have contact with other incoming aircraft.

McConnell Tower: Giant 4241 heavy, stand by.

Giant 4241 heavy: And one more thing, do you have the coordinates for the airport?

McConnell Tower: Giant 4241 heavy, stand by on that.

The coordinates they are requesting are the longitude and latitude of Beech Airport. The flight crew is definitely flustered now. It's bad enough that they landed at the wrong airport but now another doubt is starting to creep in.

McConnell Tower: Giant 4241 heavy, I have the coordinates when ready to copy.

Giant 4241 heavy: Tower ready, go ahead.

McConnell Tower: Beech is Kilo Bravo Echo Charlie, North 37 degrees 41 point 64, West 97 degrees 12 point 90.

Giant 4241 heavy: OK, let me read those back.

North 374164?

McConnell Tower: Affirmative.

Giant 4241 heavy: OK, and then East 92129… uh, zero?

McConnell Tower: *West* 97 degrees 12 point 90.

Giant 4241 heavy: Sorry about that, can't read my own handwriting, West 9212 decimal 90.

McConnell Tower: West 9712 decimal 90

Giant 4241 heavy: OK, 9712 decimal uh decimal 90.

Giant 4241 heavy: All right, here's the coordinates we're showing currently for us: North 3744 decimal 4, West 09713 decimal 3

McConnell Tower: Giant 4241 heavy, roger, stand by.

So, definitely *not* at Beech Airport. There's a long and poignant pause in the conversation.

McConnell Tower: Giant 4241 heavy…Did you do a circle around the airport and then land, or did you make it straight in?

I don't think the controller really needs the answer to that question. He's already worked out what happened.

Giant 4241 heavy: Straight in, sir.

McConnell Tower: Giant 4241 heavy, roger.

McConnell Tower: Giant 4241 heavy, can you say your coordinates again?

Giant 4241 heavy: All right, currently we are showing North 3744 decimal 4, West 09713 decimal 3. We've got a gentleman here, outside the aircraft now.

I like how he keeps saying "currently," like his coordinates might inexplicably change at any moment.

McConnell Tower: Giant 4241 heavy, roger.

Giant 4241 heavy: And sir, do you have a frequency by chance?

Because we really would like to be talking to someone at this mystery airfield where we appear to have landed.

McConnell Tower: Giant 4241 heavy, from the target we saw on the radar scope, we have you overtop, the target was overtop of Jabara airport, which is approximately 8 miles north of McConnell airport. Unicom frequency is 1 2 3 point 7, say again 1 2 3 point 7

Colonel James Jabara Airport handles general aviation and air taxi traffic. It has a single concrete runway 18/36, which is 6,101 feet (1,860 meters) long. It's named after James Jabara, an American pilot who served in World War II and the Korean War and was officially the first American jet ace.[3]

Note that the Dreamlifter needs about 7,000

---

3   https://en.wikipedia.org/wiki/Flying_ace

feet to land. The flight crew were expecting 9,000. It's actually pretty amazing that they managed to land there safely, and yet somehow they did not realise how tiny the runway was.

Giant 4241 heavy: All right, this gentleman is giving us a frequency, we're going to try it out, 1 2 3 point 7 as well.

It sounds suspiciously like some nice gentleman has walked up to the aircraft to ask the flight crew what the hell they are doing there.

Giant 4241 heavy: McConnell Tower, Giant 4241.

McConnell Tower: Giant 4241 heavy, in contact

Giant 4241 heavy: Yes sir, we are in contact with the company right now, we'll analyze for performance status.

McConnell Tower: Giant 4241 heavy, roger.

The controller doesn't sound confident that the flight crew know what they are doing... and who can blame him? They have not yet acknowledged that they are at Jabara.

McConnell Tower: Giant 4241 heavy, and confirm you know which airport you're at.

Giant 4241 heavy: Well, we think we have a pretty good pulse. Uh, how many...let me ask you this, how many airports directly to the south of 19, uh, of your 19, are there?

This was maybe not the best way to

inspire confidence.

McConnell Tower: Giant 4241 heavy, uh you're currently north of McConnell. And there's three along the approach.

Giant 4241 heavy: Sorry, I meant north. I'm sorry, I'm looking at something else. We are showing about six miles north of you.

McConnell Tower: Copy, six miles north.

The controller sounds like he just can't quite believe what's happening although he must be struggling not to laugh by now. He has tried to break it to them gently but they don't appear to be making sense of it.

McConnell Tower: And 4241 heavy, affirmative. Right now we…are still trying to figure it out.

Giant 4241 heavy: OK, thanks.

Giant 4241 heavy: Tower, we just had a twin engine aircraft, a turboprop aircraft go over the top of us.

McConnell Tower: Giant 4241 heavy, roger. It appears you are at Jabara.

Giant 4241 heavy: Uh, say again?

It's hard to resist wondering why one of the flight crew didn't simply get an iPhone out and check Google maps.

McConnell Tower: Giant 4241 heavy, we saw the plane on the radar and it appears you are at

Jabara airport.

Giant 4241 heavy: Say the name of it again?

McConnell Tower: Jabara.

Giant 4241 heavy: Jabaro?

McConnell Tower: Giant 4241 heavy, that's
J A B A R A.

Giant 4241 heavy: OK. All right. Uh, copy that.

Despite the evidence of their GPS and the gentleman who spoke to them and their coordinates and the radar display showing them as at Jabara, the flight crew is still not 100% convinced.

There is a waypoint called WARUN which is the final approach fix for the RNAV GPS approach to runway 19L; that is, they should have passed it before landing on the runway at McConnell. And this seems to sink in, that it is still in front of them.

Giant 4241 heavy: OK, we also show we are just short of, about a mile short of WARUN now.

McConnell Tower: Giant 4241 heavy, roger. Yes. That's Jabara.

Giant 4241 heavy: McConnell Tower, Giant 4241.

McConnell Tower: Giant 4241 heavy.

Giant 4241 heavy: Yes sir, it looks like we do confirm that it is Jabara.

McConnell Tower: Giant 4241 heavy, roger.

So now they know where they are. But

acceptance is only half the battle.

McConnell Tower: Giant 4241, say intentions?

Giant 4241 heavy: Uh, we're talking to the company now, we're trying to assess our performance situation as far as being able to leave this airport and come to you.

McConnell Tower: Giant 4241 heavy, roger. Just keep us advised.

Giant 4241 heavy: OK, yeah. We will not take off without clearing it through you as well.

McConnell Tower: Giant 4241 heavy, roger.

This is a serious logistical problem. The runway at Jabara is only 6,100 feet and not meant for large aircraft. The only thing they have in their favour is that they have not yet picked up their cargo, so the Dreamlifter is relatively light.

McConnell Tower: Giant 4241 heavy, McConnell Tower. Can you confirm, are you on the runway?

Giant 4241 heavy: Affirmative. I am on their Unicom frequency as well, talking to local traffic. We're trying to, uh, we're trying to assess our situation as far as clearing the runway is concerned.

McConnell Tower: Giant 4241 heavy, roger.

It's worth mentioning here that planes can't reverse and at a small aviation airport, there are no pushback tractors or tugs to push the aircraft backwards, like there are at commercial airports. So the problem isn't actually whether or not they can take off from Jabara but that they are still sitting on the runway and they can't work out how to get off of it.

Eventually, Boeing arranged for an aircraft tug to travel from McConnell to Jabara. The tug, never meant to be out on the open road, trundled along the local highway at 13 miles per hour with a police escort.

To the great relief of everyone involved, the aircraft was not heavily loaded and not carrying much fuel. It would be able to take off from the short runway. The departure the following day went seamlessly. It should be noted that a different flight crew was given the job of delivering the aircraft to McConnell. They managed to take off using only 4,500 feet of the runway after which they flew in a large circle and landed safely and at the right airport.

Where Am I Again?

ON THE 30TH of September, a 25-year-old pilot flew a Piper Super Cub to the adorably named Cuckoo Tye Farm in Suffolk to visit a friend.

The Piper Super Cub is a single engine light aircraft first produced in 1949. It has just two seats, for a pilot and a passenger, and is popular with bush fliers because of its short take-off and landing requirements. It is also cheap to insure, only requiring a private pilot licence and 50 hours flight time in a tailwheel aircraft.

On the 30th of September 2013, a 25-year old pilot flew his Piper Super Cub with a destination of Cuckoo Tye Farm to visit a friend. The aircraft did not have GPS or a mode-C transponder. He entered Stansted controlled airspace at 13:20.

You are required to have a transponder if you are flying in controlled airspace but, to be fair, he didn't *intend* to fly into controlled airspace, he just got lost. Now, it's up to the pilot to plan his navigation and to avoid controlled airspace.

However, infringements into control zones happen a lot, especially with private pilots and especially in the southeast of England, where airspace is tight.

In fact, I accidentally flew into Heathrow's control zone once, very briefly, when my autopilot unexpectedly conked out. A friendly controller from Farnham, who was watching me on his radar, contacted me to ask if everything was OK (yes, sort of) before informing me what I'd done (Oh no!) and kindly offering me a heading to get the hell out before I caused chaos (Thank you, kind soul, whoever you are).

I followed his instructions to get out of Heathrow's airspace as quickly as possible and that was the end of that. And that's the point: if you get lost and somehow find yourself close to an international airport, then your absolute priority needs to be to get out of it (navigate) and to inform air traffic control to let them know what has happened and what you are doing about it (communicate).

In this case, the pilot saw Stansted Airport and recognised it but thought—or, rather, optimistically hoped—that it was further away than it looked. He decided that rather than talk to anyone, he would fly low level and stay below the commercial traffic. It looks very much as if he hoped he could sneak past the arriving and departing jets without anyone noticing that he was there.

This was not the least bit reassuring to the Air Traffic Controllers at Stansted. They could see an unknown aircraft in their area but they didn't know anything else about it.

The airspace surrounding Stansted and Luton requires clearance to enter. Pilots can get this clearance by contacting controllers on the appropriate frequency before they reach the boundary and asking. But the pilot didn't make any attempt to contact anyone.

The controllers couldn't see that he was flying low level because he didn't have a transponder, which would have given them at least some information about him. They didn't have any contact with the pilot, because he hadn't contacted them and didn't seem to be talking to anyone.

It was his responsibility to make contact. He didn't need to know where he was to do this. A *pan pan* call can be used to declare any urgent problem. A *pan pan* call follows the same format as a Mayday call but tells the controller immediately that you are not in distress: that is, there is no immediate danger to people or the aircraft. So a pilot would use a *pan pan* call for a fuel shortage, a navigational system failure or simply to let someone know as soon as possible that he is lost. If he doesn't know whose control zone he is in, he can contact the UK Distress and Diversion cell (D&D) on 121.5 (Civil Emergencies frequency).

Because he didn't, no one knew what he was doing or at what height. While he continued his flight in silence, chaos broke out at Air Traffic Control. The controllers did the only thing they could. They stopped all departing flights and watched on radar as the Piper Super Cub drifted through Stansted and Luton airspace. He remained in controlled airspace for eleven minutes, causing a serious disruption across two major international airports in the London airspace, some of the busiest airspace in the world. Controllers could only watch (possibly peeking through their fingers) as the unknown blip passed just 1,215 feet from a Ryanair Boeing 737.

Once he was on the ground and identified, the CAA charged him with entering controlled airspace. They also determined that his five-year licence had expired, although his medical and hours were up-to-date. Considering how close he got to the heavy traffic, he was lucky that that was the worst of this escapade.

The Magistrates' Court chairman was very clear: "You knew the airspace in this part of England is very congested and therefore the burden's on you to be spot-on in your navigation." He added that the pilot knew he was lost but repeatedly failed to contact air traffic control. "While you knew what altitude you were at no-one else did, or what your intentions were. You felt safe but that's not the point."

The pilot represented himself in court. He argued that he was concentrating on his flying and navigation as per the golden rule of aviation: Aviate first, navigate second and communicate third. Clearly, his priority must be to fly the plane: it would be ludicrous to try to speak to someone if the aircraft was not under control. But, by his own account, he was flying straight and level and at low altitude to avoid possible commercial traffic, so he was fine. Having screwed up on navigation, he needed to communicate that failure, rather than continue to bumble through, hoping that he would get it sorted.

The golden rule is meant to help pilots prioritise. That doesn't mean communicating is optional.

He had not flown since the incident, he said after the hearing. "It was a frightening experience. That's why I deliberately didn't contact anyone. I was still trying to work out where I was and where I was going."

Instead, he caused a serious disruption across two major international airports who had no means of speaking to him. It was *his job* to communicate to someone what was happening, even if that was the uncomfortable admission that he had screwed up. He appears not to have grasped the fact that, although he was sure he was safe, no one else knew what he was up to, let alone that he was trying to stay under the commercial traffic and out of the way.

He pleaded guilty to infringing commercial airspace. The court levelled a fine of £3,400 (just over $4,000 US) but allowed him to keep his licence. He said he thought that the CAA was "incredibly harsh" for prosecuting him for "one navigation error."

Except that the problem was, it wasn't *just* a navigation error. It was a continuing eleven-minute-long navigation error in which he entered Stansted *and* Luton's airspace and did not contact anyone to help them work around his error. To be honest, I think he was lucky to have kept his licence.

That'll Buff Out

We all make mistakes. But when pilots have a bit of an *oops!* moment, the consequences can be catastrophic. In this section, we'll explore some of the most hilarious and outrageous pilot errors, from forgetting to release the parking brake to flying straight through the middle of another plane.

Ever Left the Parking Brake On?

ON THE 22ND of December 2017, an Embraer ERJ-145EP flew a scheduled flight from Frankfurt/Main in Germany to Bristol Airport in England. Twenty-two passengers and three crew were on board.

As the aircraft landed on runway 27, it skidded off the runway and came to a stop in the soft ground alongside. The cause? An embarrassing mistake that I suspect most car owners have done at least once: leaving the parking brake on.

The two flight crew consisted of a captain-under-training in the left-hand seat who was Pilot Flying and an airline training captain in the right-hand seat, who was the commander of the flight and who took the role of Pilot Monitoring. They reported for duty at quarter to six in the morning for the flight from Bristol Airport to Frankfurt/Main and back.

The captain-under-training was new to the airline and new to the aircraft type; he had trained on a SAAB 2000 and had just 17 hours of flight time on the Embraer 145. As Pilot Flying, he carried out a Category II approach (a precision approach using the instrument landing system), and they landed at Frankfurt without incident. Bristol was forecast for fog and during the return flight, the crew again presumed a Category II approach and that they would be landing on runway 27.

The captain-under-training started his approach briefing as they began their final descent but, as they came into range of the recorded information offering Bristol's current weather and runway conditions, he interrupted his own briefing to listen.

> Runway 27 in use, surface damp, low visibility procedures in force, surface wind variable 3 kt, visibility 150 m, Runway Visual Range (RVR) Runway 27 400 m, fog, sky obscured, temperature 10°C, dewpoint 10°C and pressure 1035 hPa.

He picked up where he left off but was interrupted again as they received additional weather information, additional instructions from air traffic control and cabin crew communications.

London Air Traffic Control instructed the aircraft to descend to FL160 (16,000 feet) and reduce speed to 250 knots. The controller also told them to expect to hold for arrival at Bristol, that is, that they wouldn't be able to route the flight in for landing immediately.

The flight crew changed frequencies to Bristol

Air Traffic Control (ATC), who confirmed that the weather conditions were acceptable for an approach. Then, to their surprise, the controller advised them that they were number one (next) for the approach. As the Embraer descended through FL140, the controller asked if 30 track miles was sufficient distance. The question was whether they could descend and configure for landing for a more direct approach which would only cover a distance of 30 miles, or if they needed more time to prepare. The crew discussed this and agreed that they could do it. They accepted the faster approach.

The captain-under-training decided that he would deploy the speedbrake to help them lose the excess height and announced "Speedbrake coming on." But according to the Flight Data Recorder, the speedbrake was not deployed.

He finally completed the approach briefing. While they checked their radio altimeters, required for the Category II approach, the commander told the captain-under-training that the quickest way to descend was to use speed mode and deploy the speedbrake. The captain-under-training acknowledged this and said that the speedbrake was already deployed, but at that moment the training captain responded to the air traffic controller on the radio and didn't seem to hear the captain-under-training.

After the call, the commander said outright that the speed brake needed to be deployed. "It is," said the captain-under-training, and then, "Oh, no, it's not. Who closed that?" He then deployed the speedbrake, confirmed by the Flight Data

Recorder, and asked the commander to request another five track-miles from ATC to give them some more time.

ATC routed the aircraft through the extended runway centreline to give them a little bit of extra distance before asking them to turn to intercept the ILS (Instrument Landing System) localiser from the south. The flight crew completed the descent checklist and the approach checklist was started.

The second item on the checklist read "SEATBELT SIGN...ON". The challenge and response system has one person, the Pilot Monitoring, reading the item and the other person, the Pilot Flying, confirming the status. Instead, for some reason, the training commander read out "PARK BRAKE." to which the captain-under-training responded "ON."

Which was correct. It was on. Somehow it didn't sink in that, under the circumstances, this was a bad thing.

At the same moment, ATC instructed the flight to descend to 2,500 feet and turn right heading 360°. The crew followed the ATC instructions and then the commander restarted the approach checklist from the beginning, this time correctly with "SEATBELT SIGN." in the second position, which the captain-under-training confirmed was ON.

At 80 feet above ground level, the captain-under-training disconnected the autopilot, ready for a manual landing.

The Embraer touched down. The main wheels locked.

The nose dropped and the aircraft slewed to the right. The captain-under-training applied opposite rudder but struggled to maintain control of the aircraft. The nose swung to the left, skidding along the centreline. The captain-under-training then applied right rudder but the aircraft continued to yaw to the left.

The commander initially thought that the trainee might be "riding the brakes". This is a common error during training and also happens in cars, where the pilot or the driver applies brake pressure throughout instead of mindfully. He told the captain-under-training to take his feet off the brakes.

On the Embraer ERJ145 (as well as the 135 and the 140), there is a steering tiller on the captain's side which allows the pilot to activate the hydraulic nosewheel steering system. The captain-under-training had been trying to use corrective rudder but as that was not allowing him to maintain directional control, he reached for the steering tiller.

The commander saw the movement. "No, no, don't use the nosewheel steering!"

He stopped the trainee pilot just in time. Normally, the tiller is used with small inputs to allow for better steering on the ground. However, it can only be used at speeds under a certain limit and is not actually meant for gaining directional control while still at high speed after landing. If the captain-under-training can't manage to steer the aircraft with the rudders, then the nosewheel tiller is not going to help. More than likely, the attempt would snap the nose-wheel strut.

Up until this point, it *might* have been possible to keep the aircraft on the runway.

The captain-under-training remembers that he also considered using asymmetric thrust to regain control but, later, he said that he didn't think that he had moved the thrust levers. However, the thrust levers *were* advanced and worse, with slightly more left thrust than right. The aircraft ran off the left side of the runway.

As the aircraft hit the grass, the commander finally realised that the parking brake was on. The aircraft fishtailed left and right on the grass, continuing another 120 metres (400 feet) before coming to a halt. The captain-under-training saw that the thrust levers had been advanced and brought them back to IDLE. Everyone took a deep breath.

God only knows what the passengers thought.

> Marks and rubber fragments on the runway defined the touchdown point, approximately 468 m from the threshold, and showed the aircraft initially tracking on the runway centreline before drifting first slightly to the right of the centreline and then veering left over 280 m.
>
> Overheated fragments of vulcanised rubber were found at various points along the runway, with a cluster of larger fragments approximately 400 m from the touchdown point over an area of approximately 40 m by 3 m. After this point there were faint but reasonably clear

lines left on the runway surface made by
the wheel rims up to the point where the
aircraft left the runway and continued
onto the grass.

All four main wheels were buried up to
their axles.

On the bright side, the aircraft was stopped and
safe and the crew agreed that there was no need
for an emergency evacuation. The commander
contacted Bristol, saying simply, "We're off the
runway." The captain-under-training made
an announcement to the cabin to reassure the
passengers that everything was fine, no really,
and to ask them to please remain seated.

The Bristol controller activated the crash alarm
and alerted the Rescue and Fire Fighting Services.

The captain-under-training realised that
he must have set the parking brake when he
originally meant to deploy the speedbrake. But
he still couldn't recall having increased the
thrust during the landing roll.

Investigators confirmed that the thrust levers
were advanced shortly before the aircraft ran off
the runway but were unable to establish if the
captain-under-training had increased them to try
to maintain directional control using asymmetric
thrust. They couldn't rule out that the additional
thrust was caused by a "biomechanical reaction"
as the aircraft decelerated.

The investigation also found that the parking
brake indicator on the centre panel was only half
lit, as one of the filaments had failed.

To be fair to the crew, when the seat is in the

forward position, the parking brake handle is not in the pilot's sight; instead, it is operated by feel. Embraer's safety case had classified the severity of *landing with the parking brake on* as major but believed that it was extremely improbable that it would ever happen. They based this on the assumption that a system fault would turn the parking brake on, which came up as having a low likelihood.

No one had even considered the possibility of the parking brake being applied while airborne.

Embraer said they only knew of two other cases of landing while the parking brake was set. They had no further details as neither case apparently warranted an investigation. The Air Accidents Investigation Branch knew of one other case, which they investigated 2007. In this case, the pilot had meant to select landing flap but set the parking brake on instead. All four main-wheel tyres deflated on landing but luckily, there was no further damage.

The intriguing thing about this mess was that the commander clearly said "park brake" instead of "seatbelt sign" when he started the checklist. This would imply that he had the park brake on his mind, possibly having seen the illuminated parking brake indicator without taking it in. If they hadn't been interrupted at that moment, one of the pilots just might have noticed the mistake and actually checked the brake.

But with all the interruptions and the desire to take the quick approach despite the higher workload, every chance to notice and fix the error was missed.

The investigation into the incident concluded that the accident was caused by the selection of the parking brake rather than the speedbrake. However, it went on to say, "After touchdown, the aircraft may have remained on the runway surface but for the addition of forward thrust during the landing roll."

The airport was closed for about thirteen hours after the incident. The aircraft, with its wheels buried in the grass, had to be lifted out of the soft ground using a combination of hydraulic jacks and airbags so that it could be towed back to the apron, the paved area where the aircraft was to be parked and inspected.

The only damage was to the landing gears and fairings.

The airline has since revised their Landing Checklist to include PARKING BRAKE...OFF.

How to Drop a Business Jet into a Ravine

Everyone involved with aviation is used to checklists. They are the cornerstone of aviation safety, meant to protect against the ever increasing complexity of aircraft and the limited attention span of the average human. They follow a pattern: a B-32 checklist from 1943 is similar in concept and design to a modern airliner checklist.

It would be nice to believe that every pilot understands the importance of checklists and why we rely on them instead of our own fallible memories, especially in times of stress.

But every so often, a flight crew decides that they don't need to follow the checklists, that they know it all, that it is just a waste of time.

This fatal accident is the result of one such crew.

It happened at Hanscom Field southwest of Bedford, Massachusetts on the 31st of May in

2014. Hanscom is primarily a general aviation airport. The primary runway, 11/29 (basically southeast/northwest) is 2,137 metres (7,011 feet) of asphalt with a slight gradient.

At the end of runway 11, there is a paved overrun area which forms a clear area beyond the runway (the runway safety area or RSA). At the end of this, there's a flat grassy area leading to the chain-link fence which marks the airport perimeter. On the other side of the fence is a ravine containing the Shawsheen River.

The total usable flat land in an emergency is 2,680 metres or 8,780 feet. After that, you will fall into the ravine.

The accident aircraft was a fourteen-year-old Gulfstream Aerospace Corporation G-IV registered in the US as N121JM. The Gulfstream IV is a twin jet with a take-off distance of 1,707 metres (5,600 feet) at sea-level. Hanscom Field is 132 feet above mean sea level.

The operator was SK Travel, who operated only the one aircraft with three staff: two pilots and one flight attendant. One of the two pilots was also the chief pilot and director of maintenance for SK travel. When one of the two pilots was not available, contract pilots were used.

The SK Travel Flight Operations Manual stated that all pilots must complete all checklists during flight operations: a standard requirement. The company did not have a flight-data monitoring program. The pilots were not regularly assessed by outside personnel for compliance with standard operating procedures. The chief pilot, who is responsible for ensuring that flight crew comply with the company's policies, was one of only two flight crew working for the company, and he was the Pilot Monitoring on the accident flight.

One of the NTSB Board Members added a statement to the final report:

> To all outward appearances, SK Travel had the hallmarks of a well-run flight department. They were operating a top-of-the-line business jet. They had long-time employment stability—something not often found with small aviation departments. They did their training at FlightSafety International instead of just trying to do it "on the cheap." The chief pilot was described as being very meticulous about the airplane's maintenance. They had undergone two voluntary industry audits and were preparing for their third audit, in itself a remarkable feat.

That day, the Gulfstream IV departed from New Castle Airport in Wilmington, Delaware at 13:25. It had an uneventful flight to Atlantic City to pick up passengers and delivered them to Hanscom Field in the late afternoon. The passengers were attending a charitable event in Bedford. The crew remained with the aircraft parked at the ramp, ready to take the passengers back to Atlantic City after the event. They did not request any maintenance or fuel services.

It was 21:28 (9:28 pm) when the passengers arrived back at Hanscom Field and boarded the aircraft. The crew started the engine at 21:30.

At 21:31:45 the flap position changed from 0° to 20°. At 21:33, the aircraft began its taxi to runway 11. The pilots discussed the taxi route and clearances as they made their way to the holding point. The chief pilot, in his role as Pilot Monitoring, confirmed that they were cleared to take-off followed by a right turn.

They turned directly onto the runway at 21:39:20 ready for departure.

Now it may not be immediately obvious what's wrong here, but from getting the passengers on board to turning onto the runway, the total elapsed time is eleven minutes.

The Gulfstream IV flight manual includes five checklists to be completed before take-off: the *Before Starting Engines* checklist, the *Starting Engines* checklist, the *After Starting Engines* checklist, the *Taxi/Before Takeoff* checklist, and the *Lineup* checklist.

Even if we presume the pilots did a walk-around before the passengers got there, there wasn't enough time to go through the *After Starting Engines* checklist in the three minutes before they started taxiing. Those checks include making sure that the brakes are working and that all the controls are free and correct.

The Cockpit Voice Recorder has no record of any conversation at all to do with checklists.

But the key reason that we know that they skipped the checklists is that neither pilot noticed that the gust lock system was still engaged.

The gust lock system is a mechanical system which locks the main control surfaces (aileron, rudder and elevators) into place in order to protect against gusting winds when the aircraft is parked.

The aircraft cannot fly when the gust lock system is engaged.

Now, according to the FAA's certification standard, if the gust lock system prevents the pilot from being able to operate the control surfaces, it must *either* automatically disengage when the pilot operates the primary flight controls *or* limit the operation of the aircraft so that the pilot receives an unmistakable warning at the start of the take-off.

An unmistakable warning is described as a warning which physically limits the operation of the aircraft in order to prevent an unsafe take-off.

When engaged, the Gulfstream-IV gust lock system restricts the operation of pilot controls (yoke, column, rudder pedals) and limits the operation of the throttle levers. The gust lock handle is painted red and when the system is engaged, the lever is "prominently adjacent" to the flap handle, the point being that the pilot's hand will make physical contact with the handle when he or she is selecting the flap position.

These features are meant to limit the operation of the aircraft and provide an unmistakable warning to the crew.

According to the certification, the throttle levers are limited to 6° if the gust lock mechanism is engaged. However, this was approved based on review of the drawings of the design and specification requirements and was not tested on the final product, by which I mean the actual aircraft.

After this accident, Gulfstream admitted that their testing showed that the current design did not, actually, meet the requirements that they thought it did. In fact, they found that the forward throttle movement allowed for three to four times more than it should have. If the throttles were pushed to the maximum allowed by the interlock, the aircraft could still achieve take-off speed, it would just take longer. About seven seconds later and about 350 metres (1,200 feet) farther down the runway than a normal take-off run.

Neither Gulfstream nor the FAA had noticed that it was possible to take off with the gust lock system engaged, leading to an aircraft in the air which the pilots could not control.

The NTS B underscored that no one from the FAA had asked for any verification testing or analysis, which would have immediately demonstrated that the throttle could be moved well beyond the 6° allowed. Instead, the FAA certified the system based on engineering drawings and Gulfstream never tested it in actuality.

Basically, it was up to the pilots to notice that the gust lock system was engaged. They've already missed the easy option, which would have been to do the *After Starting Engines* checklist.

As the aircraft turned onto the runway, the yaw damper or the rudder pedal moved the rudder control surface where it hit the restriction of the gust lock mechanism. This illuminated a warning on the control panel.

Pilot Flying: It says the rudder limit light is on.

Pilot Monitoring: What's that?

Pilot Flying: The rudder limit light is on.

Pilot Monitoring: Are you using your rudders?

Pilot Flying: No.

Pilot Monitoring: Huh.

That was the second chance to realise that the gust lock mechanism was blocking the rudder pedal, or at least to take seriously the issue that the rudder's movement was limited.

Instead, they continued onto the runway and increased the power for their ground roll.

Normally, the pilot would advance the throttle levers to an angle of around 30° which would give them an engine power ratio (EPR) of about 1.7 for the take-off roll before engaging the auto-throttle.

Because the gust lock system was engaged, the throttle lever was restricted to about 50% of the normal range of movement. The levers stopped at 17.5°, achieving an engine power ratio of about 1.42, where it remained for about five seconds.

The Pilot Flying can't quite make sense of what is happening. The statements in parentheses were not clear on the Cockpit Voice Recorder.

Pilot Flying: Couldn't get (it manually any further).

Pilot Monitoring: Eighty.

Pilot Monitoring: V-1.

Pilot Monitoring: Rotate.

This would normally have been a good time to abort the take-off, as the Pilot Flying is clear that he couldn't push the throttles forward as expected. But instead, the Pilot Monitoring, who is the Chief Pilot of the airline, simply continues with his call-outs for a normal take off.

V1 is the "take-off decision speed", the point at which the pilots should decide whether to continue or abort the take off. Vr or *Rotate* means the aircraft has reached the speed where the pilot begins to pitch up. As the aircraft reaches take-off speed and the nose wheel comes off the ground, the aircraft will lift off from the runway.

The Pilot Flying never checked the elevator for freedom of movement (Pro-tip: it had none). He also failed to notice that the control yoke, which should have moved slightly as they gathered speed, was being held firmly in place by the gust lock mechanism.

Instead, he engaged the autothrottle.

It's unclear what he was thinking. The NTSB investigators theorised that he understood that the throttle lever was restricted and thought he could force the levers forward with the help of the autothrottle.

What actually seems to have happened is that the lock pin in the gust lock handle broke under the pressure. The throttle levers suddenly moved forward and the aircraft reached something pretty close to take-off speed. But only the throttle levers were working again, the gust lock system was still engaged, locking the rest of the control surfaces as the Gulfstream IV continued to barrel down the runway.

When the Pilot Flying attempted to rotate, he discovered that he couldn't move the control yoke. He finally grasped what was wrong and called out that the lock was on.

They'd already passed the V1 go or no-go decision point at which point aborting is dangerous. However, the aircraft simply cannot fly with the gust lock on. The only possible option is to abort the take-off and hope the aircraft stops in time.

In this particular instance, where they hadn't actually quite reached normal speeds, it would have been enough.

If this were a simple case of not following the checklist, this chapter would end right here. Having realised that the aircraft was in no state to fly, the flight crew could have stopped the aircraft and dealt with the problem.

Pilot Flying: (Steer) lock is on.

Pilot Flying: (Steer) lock is on.

Pilot Flying: (Steer) lock is on.

Pilot Flying: (Steer) lock is on.

Cockpit Area Microphone: [sounds similar to thump and squeak]

Pilot Flying: (Steer) lock is on.

Pilot Flying: (Steer) lock is on.

Pilot Flying: (Steer) lock is on.

The Pilot Monitoring did not acknowledge.

Rather than abort the take-off, one of the pilots, or possibly both, attempted to disengage the gust lock as they continued travelling at speed down the runway.

They activated the *flight power shutoff valve*. Activating the flight power shutoff valve removes hydraulic pressure from the actuators for the spoilers and the primary flight controls. This is intended to counteract a flight control actuator malfunction. The ailerons, elevator and rudder revert to manual operation when the flight power shutoff valve is activated.

This doesn't fix the problem that the ailerons, elevators and rudder were locked into place; however, it was a well-known hack for moving the gust lock handle if it was stuck.

A Gulfstream IV pilot interviewed by investigators explained that relieving the hydraulic pressure by using the flight power shutoff valve could allow the gust lock handle to be moved to the OFF position if it had stopped in an intermediate position as a result of a hydraulic load on one of the gust lock hooks. That is, if the gust lock system did not fully disengage, activating the flight power shutoff valve could help to get it into the OFF position.

This usage is not approved by Gulfstream; however when they tested the hack, they agreed that, if the aircraft was parked or taxiing at low speed, it could allow the gust lock handle to be moved if stuck.

However, the Gulfstream IV was not travelling at low speed. At the point that they activated the flight power shut off valve, the aircraft was travelling at 150 knots.

Even if the action *had* relieved the hydraulic

pressure, the hand force required to push the handle forward and disengage the elevator gust lock hook at 150 knots would be about 189 pounds, the equivalent of bench pressing a large kangaroo, if the kangaroo were a small handle that could only be pushed with one hand.

One of the pilots attempted to push the handle to the OFF position but he never had a chance.

Human factors research shows that a flight crew confronted with a sudden abnormal event will have a delayed response. Reaction times of 8 to 10 seconds may not be unusual. But the problem here was not that they reacted too slowly but that their reaction was completely *wrong*.

If they had aborted their take-off when the Pilot Flying first announced that the lock was on, they would have come to a complete and safe stop still on the runway. Instead of rejecting the take-off, the flight crew appear to have concluded that whatever was wrong, they could fix it quickly during the take-off roll and still get away on time.

The attempt to disengage the lock by operating the flight power shutoff valve took place six seconds after the Pilot Flying first called out that the lock was on.

If he'd decided to reject the take-off at that point, six seconds after his first call-out, he *still* could have stopped the aircraft safely. In fact, he had eleven seconds after that call-out to initiate the rejected take-off, and they still would have stopped on the paved surface.

At the ten second point, the flight data recorder shows that the left and right brake pressures began to rise. Here was the decision to abort the take-off, and just in time. But the two pilots weren't communicating with each other, and they were still distracted by trying to disengage the gust lock while the aircraft was rolling. It was four seconds later that the throttle levers were pulled back.

That was too late.

Worse, because they had successfully activated the flight power shut off valve, the ground spoilers did not automatically deploy to offer enhanced braking action.

Fifteen seconds after his first announcement that the locks were engaged, four seconds after his final chance to abort the take-off safely, the Pilot Flying said, "I can't stop it." He was right.

His last words were "Oh no. No." as the aircraft broke through the perimeter fence.

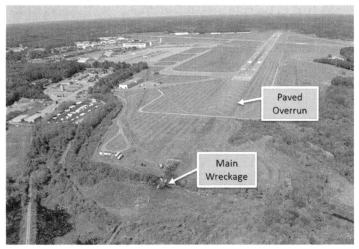

Aerial view after the crash

The skid marks from the brakes started 425 metres (1,400 feet) from the end of the runway and continued a total of 730 metres (2,400 feet) to the end of the paved overrun area.

Here, the ground sloped down slightly to a small service road. The three wheels dug into the grass just after the road and the nose gear assembly was found at the end of a rut about 25 metres (85 feet) long. Three approach light structures and the localizer antenna were knocked down and broken. The ruts from the main gear continued on. The airport's chain-link perimeter fence was knocked down and the tail of the Gulfstream IV came to rest on the airport side of the ravine. The engines, wings and fuselage were in the ravine with the cockpit on the far side.

A fire erupted immediately.

Air Traffic Control heard the Pilot Flying saying, "I can't stop it," and saw the aircraft hurtling towards the ravine. The Hanscom Air Force Base Fire Department were notified just nine seconds later and the first vehicle left the station within a minute and a half of the alert.

They reported smoke in the air and a visible fire near the end of runway 11.

A minute later, the first firefighting vehicle reached the overrun area and another three departed the fire station. The aircraft was engulfed in flames and the ravine shielded the fire. They did not know how to get across and the airport grid map did not show the location of the perimeter gate needed to access the east side of the ravine. It was an hour and 47 minutes before they were able to control the fire and attempt to gain entry to the Gulfstream. It was much too late.

Based on the position of the pilots and the passengers, we know that they survived the initial impact; however the fire burnt so fast and furiously that they were not able to make it to the exit of the aircraft. Cause of death for six of the seven occupants was smoke inhalation and thermal injuries.

Investigators determined that even if the firefighting crew had been able to get to both sides of the ravine immediately and more quickly gain control of the fire, it would have been too late.

The black box showed that the pilots had skipped the checklists that evening, presumably tired and just wanting to get home. But when the NTSB continued to review the data, they discovered something worse. This was not an isolated event.

The Gulfstream IV's quick access recorder had 303 hours of data stored on a removable compact flash card. This data included 176 take-offs, including the accident take-off.

The NTSB reviewed the data looking for evidence of a complete or partial control check before take-off, that is, a simple action of moving the elevators, ailerons and rudder to show that the three primary flight controls were able to move from stop to stop, the most basic test before take-off.

In all 176 recorded take-off events, the NTSB only found two complete control checks, and sixteen partials. The most recent partial control check (stop-to-stop movement of the elevators

and ailerons but not the rudder) was performed
12 flights before the accident.

From the accident report:[4]

3.2 Probable Cause

The NTSB determines that the probable
cause of this accident was the flight
crewmembers' failure to perform the
flight control check before takeoff,
their attempt to take off with the gust
lock system engaged, and their delayed
execution of a rejected takeoff after they
became aware that the controls were
locked.

Contributing to the accident were the
flight crew's habitual noncompliance
with checklists, Gulfstream Aerospace
Corporation's failure to ensure that the
G-IV gust lock/throttle lever interlock
system would prevent an attempted
takeoff with the gust lock engaged, and
the Federal Aviation Administration's
failure to detect this inadequacy during
the G-IV's certification.

It's true that if Gulfstream had limited
the power throttle as originally specified, the
aircraft would never have gathered enough
speed to go hurtling across the grass and into the
ravine. Nevertheless, the manufacturer cannot
safeguard against all eventualities. The flight

---

4   https://www.ntsb.gov/investigations/Pages/ERA-
14MA271.aspx

crew were complacent. The airline did not set up checks and balances to halt the normalisation of deviance. Over time, both flight crew decided that it was fine to skip the checklists. Soon, they rarely even bothered to check that the controls were free and correct. Their casual attitude was already leading inexorably to an accident. Even knowing all this, the very idea that they would continue the take-off run with the control surfaces locked simply beggars belief.

Mid-Air Collision on Approach

Centennial Airport is a busy general aviation airport in Denver, Colorado. Centennial has three asphalt runways: the parallel runways 17L/35R, 17R/35L and a third runway nearly perpendicular to the others (10/28).

On the 11th of May 2021, a Cirrus SR-22 and a Swearingen Metroliner collided while on approach to land at Centennial Airport.

At the time of the incident, the parallel southbound runways 17 left and 17 right were in use.

The Swearingen Metroliner is a twin turboprop, popular as a business aircraft. The Metroliner that day, a 43-year-old SA226-TC registration N280KL, was an air charter cargo flight operating as Key Lime Air flight 970. The pilot was the only occupant for the repositioning flight from Salida, Colorado to Centennial Airport.

The Cirrus SR-22 is a high tech single engine aircraft which is known for its full aircraft parachute system. The private light aircraft was owned by a local flight school and rental firm. The private pilot had rented the aircraft for a local area flight. The Cirrus had two on board, the pilot and one passenger, and was returning to Centennial Airport after an hour's flight in the Fort Collins area in the foothills of the Rocky Mountains.

The weather was clear and the visibility was good. The Metroliner was inbound from the north and cleared for a straight-in approach to runway 17L, the longest of the runways at Centennial with 10,000 feet (3,048 metres). He was descending through 6,400 feet about three nautical miles north of the runway threshold.

At the same time, the Cirrus was coming in from the northwest and speaking on a different ATC frequency. He was cleared for a visual approach to runway 17R, a shorter runway parallel to the first. He was advised to watch for traffic landing on the parallel runway and warned not to veer too far to the east.

He agreed that he had the traffic in sight.

If we could rise straight up into the air and look down at the airport, we would have seen the Metroliner travelling south, with a straight in approach to the left-hand runway. The Cirrus, flying slightly higher than the Metroliner, would first appear in our view directly west of the airport. It set up for an approach by turning left to head north, and then right, heading east to intercept the runway centerline. Once the pilot spotted the runway, another right turn to the south should bring him onto final approach, lined up perfectly for the right-hand runway.

It's important that he make that turn onto the centreline for the right-hand runway, otherwise he is going to drift into the way of the Metroliner coming in for the left-hand runway.

The Cirrus initiated a gentle turn towards the south, but as he descended through 6,400 feet, he missed the turn onto final, crossing the centrelines of both runway 17R and 17L.

The Tower controller reacted immediately.

Controller: Cirrus 6 Delta Juliet...Did you overshoot the final?

He must have seen the two blips come together on his radar as he didn't wait for an answer.

Controller: Cirrus 6 Delta Juliet, do you require assistance?

The Metroliner pilot never saw the Cirrus. All he knew was that something bad had just happened as his aircraft suddenly lurched to the left. He immediately declared an emergency.

Metroliner: We had, um...looks like the right engine failed so I'm going to continue my landing.

The pilot of the Cirrus obviously also did not see the Metroliner until it was too late, even though he had called that he had the traffic in sight. He would have been looking out of his right window to find the runway as he made that final turn and presumably didn't see the airfield either.

A third aircraft, a Cessna 172 whose pilot was flying his first solo, was inbound to the same runway. He was keeping the Cirrus in sight as the "traffic to follow": the aircraft in front of him in the circuit. He saw the Cirrus deploy its parachute. Knowing that was never a good sign, he reported this to the air traffic control, who quickly asked for a more specific location. The controller made another call to the Cirrus, hoping that the message might get through.

Controller: Cirrus 6 Delta Juliet, if you hear this transmission, we have emergency vehicles in your direction.

The Metroliner continued its approach and landed safely on runway 17R. After landing, the pilot called the controller.

Metroliner: Tower, that was definitely a mid-air on short final.

Yes, it sure was.

Photograph of the Metroliner after the accident

The centre of the Metroliner had been carved out as if with a can opener, exposing the cabin.

I'm not sure it had really sunk in, however, as when the pilot was asked if he needed assistance, he replied cool as a cucumber.

Metroliner: I'm going to taxi off here and I think I'll just park over at Signature. I'm good, though.

A local resident heard the collision. "I was in the kitchen and I heard a loud firecracker bang. I ran out I thought, 'Is it somebody jumping out of a plane?' And then I realised the parachute was attached to a plane."

Another resident ran to the scene expecting the worst and was stunned when he saw two men, the pilot and his passenger, in front of the Cirrus SR-22, which seemed to be broken in two. The men were unharmed. "They were just standing there like they were at a cocktail party," he said.

Amazingly, no one was injured. The local sheriff quipped that both pilots should buy lottery tickets immediately.

The pilot of the Cessna 172 made a drawing to commemorate his first solo flight. Drawn with marker pen onto the fabric of his T-shirt, it shows a childlike sketch of a plane flying over a runway with, below, an orange parachute attached to an aircraft. The words "traffic to follow" are written with an arrow pointing at the parachute. There is a single fluffy cloud.

The NTSB have confirmed that they are investigating.

How Will We Stop the Engine, Then?

You MAY HAVE SEEN the shocking photographs in the news in 2009, when an aircraft crashed through the wall of an airport building, killing one passenger.

The CRJ100 had just taken off from Kigali International Airport when the flight crew declared an emergency as they were experiencing a fault with the throttle. They returned to Kigali and landed safely.

At the time, all we knew was that the ground crew were in the process of placing chocks in front of the wheels of the stopped aircraft when it suddenly accelerated. The aircraft veered to the right and proceeded straight through numerous blast fences before crashing into the VIP lounge.

Sylvia Wrigley

Challenger embedded in the wall of the VIP lounge

The business jet was a Bombardier Challenger, specifically a CRJ100 in the Bombardier CL-600-2B19 series. The Challenger was owned and operated by Jetlink, who had acquired the aircraft in June 2007, two years earlier. The Challenger 600 had two Avco Lycoming ALF 502 geared turbofan engines.

The flight was RwandAir WB205, a scheduled international flight from Kigali International Airport to Entebbe in Uganda. Jetlink Express Limited was operating the flight on behalf of RwandAir. On that day, the 12th of November 2009, ten passengers and five crew were on board, including one flight engineer.

The aircraft took off normally at 12:54. During the initial take-off climb, the flight crew found that the thrust lever for the number one engine (on the left side) had jammed. They could not reduce the engine throttle at all, thus the left-hand engine was still producing take-off power. The captain notified air traffic control and entered a holding pattern. Meanwhile, the first officer requested the help of a company flight engineer who was travelling on the flight, and the two of them attempted to reduce the power to the engine.

After it became clear that they could not unjam the throttle, the captain notified Kigali that they were returning. After one go-around, the Challenger successfully landed on runway 28 and taxied towards the parking bay before turning and accelerating into the VIP lounge.

At the time, the acting chief executive of RwandAir said they had no idea how this could have happened. He said that their best guess was that the aircraft auto-accelerated, whatever that might mean.

"The captain could not control it. The plane did not get airborne again, it taxied into the building. The captain was taken to the hospital with a broken leg. He has not been able to give us any information so far."

The Director-General of the Rwandan Civil Aviation Authority did not have any better explanation.

"For some unexplained reason, the plane, from the parking spot, took off again at full power and...took a right turn, unexplained, into the technical building,"

A week later, RwandAir made a statement[5] but

5   http://www.eturbonews.com/12766/statement-rwandair-re-

they simply repeated the same nonsense, adding that the flight crew had been tested for substance abuse. They were entirely sober. None of this did anything to explain how the CRJ100 had simply run away like that. Yes, the throttle was still jammed but having successfully landed and taxied to the parking bay, why on earth would the aircraft then suddenly accelerate from a standing stop?

The flight crew didn't have any good answers.

The captain:

> ... after getting airborne, I asked my
> copilot to conduct the climb and after
> takeoff checks. She had a problem with
> retarding the left thrust lever. I called
> the engineer to help the copilot retard
> the left throttle, but it was not possible. I
> asked the tower controller for permission
> to land. I landed with one engine on
> maximum power and landed normally
> though heavy braking, the tires deflated
> and parked the aircraft and shortly the
> plane started rolling downwards toward
> the barrier and Air Traffic Control Tower
> building. I had no control over the plane as
> I even tried to steer it clear of the building.

The first officer:

> ... after takeoff, I tried to set climb thrust
> and noticed the left thrust lever could not
> adjust. I then informed the captain that

garding-aircraft-crashing-kigali-internatio

the throttle was stuck. He tried to adjust
it too but it was stuck. We then called for
the engineer, we coordinated together
and the captain focused on flying the
plane safely while I communicated with
ATC, did the checklists and we combined
efforts with the engineer to try and adjust
the left thrust lever. We landed safely and
parked but the left thrust lever could not
be adjusted still. As we were trying to
retard it and shut it down while holding
on brakes, the plane started rolling again.
Efforts to stop it from rolling failed but the
captain managed to control it away from
the other traffic. We then hit a wall as the
plane could not stop and the thrust lever
was still stuck forward.

Now to be fair, it's clearly not the pilots' fault
that the throttle got stuck. But they had it under
control, it seemed, until suddenly they didn't.
What happened?

The Republic of Rwanda Ministry of
Infrastructure initiated an investigation but it
took them eight years to release their report and
unravel the mystery for the rest of us.

First, let's go over the exact sequence of events.

On the Cockpit Voice Recorder, we can hear
that the captain and the first officer realised that
the thrust lever was sticking during the take-
off roll. They decided to continue. The aircraft
took off normally with the number one engine
at 94% power and the number two engine at
91% power. As they climbed away, the number

2 engine decreased to 69% while the number 1 engine remained at 94%. The first officer tried to reduce the power for the climb but to no avail.

They asked an engineer to come forward from the cabin. The engineer looked at the left throttle but wasn't able to fix it. The captain informed the passengers that there was a fault and that the flight was returning to Kigali.

At this point, the number 1 engine power increased to 97%, much too high for an aircraft in the cruise.

The CRJ100 began its descent. Power for the number 1 engine reduced to 96% and the number 2 engine reduced to 32%. Over the next few minutes, the power of the number 2 engine varied between 88% and 27% while the number 1 engine remained steady at around 95%.

The flight crew circled to lose altitude and the captain set up the aircraft for the approach and landing, while the first officer and the engineer continued to try to reduce the power to the number 1 engine. The captain told them that he was concerned that the engine might overheat.

But no one had any idea how to deal with the stuck throttle and no one seemed to consider that they might look it up. They had access to the quick reference handbook, the flight crew operating manual and the aircraft's flight manual. There are very clear checklists and systems for dealing with a stuck throttle. At no point did anyone say that maybe they should check for the correct procedure. Neither did anyone mention that they could contact operations on the ground and ask.

Instead, they continued the descent. The flight

landed safely on the runway, with the number 1 engine at 95% power and the number 2 engine at 27%. The crew continued to discuss the issue as they taxied to the stand. The full transcript was not released, unfortunately, but an excerpt makes it clear that they had no idea what to do.

First Officer: How will we stop the engine, then?

Captain: We'll just think it over. It's a problem.

We'll just think it over. The concept of looking it up or asking the maintenance team for advice apparently never occurred to them.

A warning sounded through the cockpit and the first officer called out the cause: brake overheat.

The captain stopped the aircraft at the stand and shut down the right engine. They called the Senior Cabin Crew member to the flight deck. They explained that the left-hand engine couldn't be shut down, so they would have to disembark the passengers on the right side, through the galley door. The captain said not to open the door yet. "Relax until I give you the green light."

The senior cabin crew member returned to the cabin and asked the passengers to remain seated and unfasten their seat belts.

That's when the crew noticed that the aircraft was moving. The ground speed quickly increased to 23 knots (26 mph, 42 km/h). The pilots shouted for the engineer to come back to the cockpit. At the same time, the senior cabin crew member preparing for the evacuation at the right side saw that they were moving at a fast speed. Fearful that they might crash, he and the engineer both rushed to the front seats and braced behind the bulkhead.

The captain shouted for the chocks to be placed. It was much too late for that.

The remainder of the cockpit voice recording is the screams of the passengers and the crashing sounds as the aircraft crashed into the VIP lounge.

The CRJ100 shuddered to a stop, embedded in the wall. The cabin crew opened the overwing emergency exists. The left hand engine was still running, so the cabin crew led the passengers out of the cabin over the right-hand wing. One passenger was trapped unconscious underneath the galley area. Cabin crew carried her out of the wreckage and she was quickly taken to hospital.

The captain and the first officer were trapped in the cockpit as the flight instrument panel collapsed on top of them. The captain was able to pull himself out from under. The first officer struggled but could not free herself.

Close by, a second aircraft had just finished boarding. Unsure what was happening, they evacuated their passengers as well.

A witness on the ground saw the aircraft strike the wind barriers and watched in horror as it sped towards the building. After the crash, the fire trucks arrived and sprayed water into the engine intake, but the engine continued to run. The witness forced his way into the cockpit where he found the first officer trapped under the collapsed instrument panel.

Ten minutes had passed since the crash and the engine was still running. He searched the panel for fire shut-off valves when suddenly he realised that both the left and right throttles were in the maximum and full-power positions. He pulled the throttles back to the shutdown position. The engine shut down.

It took rescue personnel three hours to free the first officer from the wreckage. Meanwhile, an ambulance swiftly took the captain, the engineer and two passengers to the hospital. On the way, they were involved in a traffic accident and a pedestrian was killed.

The pilots are not to blame for the stuck throttle. The fault had been introduced eleven days before the accident. An aircraft engineer from Europe was hired to supervise the CRJ100 as it underwent routine maintenance in the hanger.

As a part of the maintenance, staff needed to access the number 1 engine, which meant that they needed to open the cowling. Now the aircraft engineer was absolutely certain that, after the maintenance, he had personally closed the cowl door, including stowing and securing the cowl strut. It's impossible to prove whether or not he did so correctly, although he was adamant that he had. He suspected that the engine cowl doors had been opened again after this maintenance had concluded.

That said, the aircraft engineer wasn't a stickler for details: he definitely failed to secure a rod on the fuel control unit. When they ran the ground tests for the left engine, the rod came loose, making it impossible to control the engine. He had to cut off the fuel in order to shut down the engine.

A week later, the CRJ100 had completed the

scheduled routine maintenance. On the first flight after the maintenance, two days before the accident, the aircraft had to turn back, reporting a generator problem on the number 1 engine. Maintenance staff resolved the issue and the aircraft was returned to service the same day.

We don't know whether the cowling door was opened as a part of this but at some point in the eleven days before the accident flight, someone had neglected to stow the upper core cowl support rod. The support rod had a pin which needed to be inserted in order to keep the rod in place but that pin was still hanging from its lanyard.

The CRJ100 had flown 4.6 hours, during which the vibrations from the engine slowly shifted the strut until it was blocking the fuel control unit actuating arm. Now it was impossible to reduce the power of the left-hand engine to less than 93%.

This was the cause of the stuck engine throttle.

It wasn't the first time that this had happened: Transport Canada published the details of eight incidents involving a thrust lever jam of the left engine for the Bombardier Challenger. Bombardier had issued eight service bulletins between August 2000 and January 2009 warning operators that incorrect stowage of the support rod could lead to the rod working its way free and falling between the engine fuel control unit and the throttle control gearbox.

However, the risk of an in-flight throttle jam was considered low. As a result, the recommended modifications in the service bulletins were categorised as "discretionary for compliance". Bombardier updated the Aircraft

Flight Manual and the Flight Crew Operations Manual with clear procedures for dealing with a *Throttle Lever Jammed* event.

The airline had complied with the initial service bulletins but had disregarded the most recent one. The maintenance personnel knew how to properly stow the engine and cowl, but when investigators followed up, they found that the engineers didn't know about the service bulletins and that they didn't understand the risk of a jammed thrust lever.

The basics of the incidents documented by Transport Canada were the same as what had happened that day in Kigali, with one big difference. In every other case, the aircraft landed and parked without further incident. Only in this one case did the aircraft "auto-accelerate" once on the ground.

The difference was quite simply the experience and ability of the flight crew.

It's not just that they didn't know how to handle the jammed thrust lever, they literally did not know how to deal with a situation where they didn't know what to do.

The Aircraft Flight Manual and the Flight Crew Operations Manual had been updated with clear instructions for the Throttle Lever Jammed procedure. Of course, that only helps if someone bothers to read it.

As soon as they were aware that the throttle was stuck, one of the flight crew should have been checking the operational manual. Instead, they struggled through the landing with one engine at full power.

In every other jammed throttle lever incident documented, the flight crew pressed the FIRE/ PUSH button to shut down the left-hand engine. They then landed on one engine, which was working correctly.

The fact that this flight crew managed to land the aircraft safely with one engine on full power is actually somewhat amazing, except for the fact that it was a problem of their own making.

Having taxied to the stand, the flight crew must have believed that the worst of it was over. The captain became completely focused on evacuating the passengers, which is why he had the cabin crew ask them to unbuckle their safety belts directly before the impact.

But the engine was still running at full power and the brakes were overheating. Neither pilot mentioned setting the parking brake and according to the Flight Data Recorder (FDR) it was not set, although after the crash, the brake was found in the engaged position. At some point, the left tyre had deflated. The captain thought that this had happened on landing, although, equally, it could have deflated as the brake overheat warning sounded in the cockpit. The tyre could also have ruptured at the last minute from the high temperatures of the hot brakes.

In any event, once the left tyre was flat, there was no traction for the brake pressure. Even if the parking brake was set, it couldn't have stopped the aircraft. The left tyre would have been dragged across the ramp without the brakes doing anything at all.

The point is that while the flight crew sat

in the cockpit discussing the evacuation, the brakes were burning up. They'd shut down the right-hand engine, which reduced the hydraulic pressure, but seemed unconcerned that the left-hand engine was still running at full power. Finally, the brakes failed completely and the aircraft, powered by the left-hand engine running at 95%, began to rumble forward.

The only braking power they had left was on the right inside tyre, forcing the CRJ 100 to veer hard to the right as it began to move. It quickly accelerated, crashing through the jet blast barrier and into the VIP lounge.

The final investigation report concluded that the probable cause of this crash was the flight crew's failure to identify corrective action. Yes, the jammed throttle was the inciting incident, however, if the flight crew had checked their manuals—as is standard procedure—or even belatedly reacted to the warning that the brakes were overheating, they could have avoided the disaster. They had ample time to find a solution.

The stuck throttle was an inconvenience, not an emergency. The mistakes that caused this tragedy were surprisingly simple: the flight crew didn't know how to shut down the engine and never considered that they should look up the answer or ask for engineers on the ground for advice. The root of the accident is encapsulated in the exchange on the flight deck.

First Officer: How will we stop the engine, then?

Captain: We'll just think it over. It's a problem.

It is clearly a case of pilot error but we should also consider the airline that allowed the two pilots to assume command of a passenger plane. This flight crew simply did not have even the basic knowledge and skills they needed to handle an emergency.

Unsafe Sex

Sex in the Cockpit isn't all it's cracked up to be. They say that sex sells, but when it comes to flying, it can also be deadly. In this section, we'll look at the hilarious and tragic consequences of pilots who engage in risky behaviour, from sex in the cockpit to dangerous stunts that end in disaster.

Activities Not Related To the
Conduct of This Flight

SOMETIMES, I SIMPLY HAVE nothing to add. This is the NTSB report after the aircraft crashed in Florida, killing both pilots.

> **NTSB Identification:** MIA92FA051. The docket is stored on NTSB microfiche number 46312.

> **14 CFR Part 91:** General Aviation Accident occurred Monday, December 23, 1991 in Rainbow Lake, FL.

> **Aircraft:** Piper PA-34-200T

> **Injuries:** 2 Fatal.

The private pilot and a pilot-rated passenger were going to practice simulated instrument flight. Witnesses observed the airplane's right wing fail in a dive and crash. Examination of the wreckage and bodies revealed that both occupants were partially clothed and the front right seat was in the full aft reclining position. Neither body showed evidence of seatbelts or shoulder harnesses being worn. Examination of the individuals' clothing revealed no evidence of ripping or distress to the zippers and belts.

The National Transportation Safety Board determines the probable cause(s) of this accident as follows:

The pilot in command's improper in-flight decision to divert her attention to other activities not related to the conduct of the flight. Contributing to the accident was the exceeding of the design limits of the airplane leading to a wing failure.

Interfering With Helicopter Controls

THE CASE OF the Federal Aviation Authority against the pilot started when the FAA revoked the pilot's commercial certificate under 14 CFR 91.13: Careless or reckless operation of an aircraft. The pilot appealed the revocation with the NTSB.

Such an appeal gives him the chance to file an answer, admitting or denying each of the allegations in the FAA complaint. A hearing is held with an Administrative Law Judge, who conducts a formal hearing and issues initial decisions on appeals by airmen. His decision will affirm, reverse or modify the FAA's action.

The NTSB serves as the "court of appeals" for any airman, mechanic or mariner whenever certificate action is taken by the Federal Aviation Administration or the US

Coast Guard Commandant, or when civil
penalties are assessed by the FAA.

—from the NTSB site[6]

A second appeal can then be made to the full board, which can affirm, modify or reverse the judge's decision or remand the case for further proceedings.

If the Board affirms the FAA's action then the certificate holder can make a third appeal, this time to the US District Court or the US Court of Appeals.

So the FAA filed an Emergency Order of Revocation to rescind the Airman Certificate from the man whom I will refer to as the pilot because Pilot Flying doesn't seem quite right and every other quick reference term I could use for the guy is probably not suitable for younger readers.

Specifically, he was the Pilot in Command of a Bell 206B helicopter during a passenger-carrying flight around San Diego, California in 2005, four years earlier.

The case was heard in 2009 by an administrative law judge for the NTSB, whose job it was to issue a bench decision as to how the law (in this case, § 91.13(a)) applied to that flight in San Diego.

Two passengers were on the flight, a woman sitting in the front and a man in the back. The issue was that during the flight, the passenger in the front seat had leaned over the collective pitch control of the helicopter to perform a sex act on the pilot.

There was no question that the, um, event

---

6   https://www.ntsb.gov/legal/alj/Pages/default.aspx

had happened, as the passenger in the rear seat had recorded the whole thing on his video camera. The initial incident had escaped the FAA's notice but when the video went viral on the internet four years later, the FAA pulled the pilot's commercial certificate.

The judge summed up the video evidence:

> And during this flight, Respondent received an oral sex act by a partially nude young lady. I say young lady; it appeared to be a young lady. Those things become relative, as I get older, but it appeared to be a young lady who was in the left seat of the helicopter and it was being videoed by someone unidentified, who was in the backseat. And the young lady was never identified either.

The young lady was in fact identified by the press as a well-known Swedish porn star but I guess "well-known" is also relative. She told the press that the "in-flight entertainment" was compensation for the pilot allowing his helicopter to be used in a porn film shot in a hangar.

Anyway, after the video went viral, the FAA alleged that a careless or reckless act had taken place and revoked the pilot's Airman Certificate on an emergency basis.

When the case was heard, the pilot was happy to admit all of the acts alleged by the FAA. The only portion of the complaint that he denied was that it was a careless and reckless act. His defence was that, under the circumstances, revoking his licence was inappropriate.

So that was the question for the judge: was receiving oral sex while being in command of a Bell 206 twin-engined helicopter flying over a major city careless or reckless?

The FAA brought an aviation safety inspector as a witness to review the video recording and to give his expert opinion as to whether it showed reckless conduct.

The expert witness pointed out that the video shows that the flight was over a populated area. He explained the importance of a helicopter pilot not being distracted during flight. He explained the helicopter controls (the collective, the cyclic and the tail rotor anti-torque pedals) and that, in an emergency, the pilot needed to be able to manipulate these controls without interference from his own clothing and without interference from the passenger's body.

Even a musty old court document can't quite help but sound salacious in these circumstances.

The pilot and the passenger had unfastened their seat belts and shoulder harnesses, which would mean that any sudden manoeuvre could throw either or both of them against the controls. The expert witness concluded that the operation of the aircraft was reckless because the pilot's access to the controls was restricted and that the control of the aircraft was jeopardised by the location of the pilot's clothing (by which I assume the witness meant his trousers around his knees) and the position of the passenger's body.

The judge recapped this narrative in his judgement.

And there were several aspects of it that he pointed out. Among them was that the Respondent had unbuckled his seatbelt, his shoulder harness was obviously loose, as depicted in that. His trousers, jeans, were down almost to his knees and appeared to be up against the cyclic. And the young lady was leaning over the collective. I'm not a helicopter pilot; I hope I get those controls right. But the up and down control, she was over that.

The up-and-down control is the collective. I have to admit, I'm struggling to find imagery for this chapter which isn't suggestive.

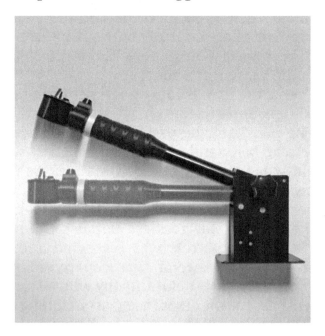

Bell 206 Collective

126

The judge desperately did not want to have to describe what the pilot had done repeatedly so after this explanation, he simply referred to "the incident that was shown in the video tape" as a sort of polite shorthand as the proceedings continued.

The witness for the FAA pointed out that any number of things could have gone wrong at that moment, ranging from turbulence to an engine failure, which could easily have caused the pilot to lose control of the aircraft. On cross-examination, the FAA witness conceded that none of those things occurred on that evening but that the case was about the potential for loss of control. He also testified that the pilot had a prior history of offences: his private pilot's licence had been revoked in 1986 and his commercial pilot certificate had been revoked in 2004 and then suspended in 2006 (after the flight in question but for a different incident). Under the circumstances, this was a serious enough violation to justify the FAA action.

The pilot argued that, as nothing *had* gone wrong, what he had done was not reckless. Further, he explained that he was a competent helicopter pilot and that in the intervening four years, he'd become even more responsible.

The pilot obviously couldn't deny the position of the passenger or the state of his undress, there being video of it and all. Instead, he defended himself by calling three witnesses, all three of whom stated that he was a skilled helicopter pilot.

The first was a commercial helicopter pilot who worked for the pilot's company. He said that he believed the pilot had the care, judgement and responsibility required to hold the certificate. However, he agreed that the video perhaps didn't demonstrate that care, judgement and responsibility.

The second witness was a private helicopter pilot and a friend of the pilot's. He said he had flown with the pilot a number of times and that he felt comfortable flying with him.

The third witness, a certified flight instructor, had flown over 200 hours with the pilot. He also felt that the pilot had the care, judgement and responsibility required but conceded that there was a time several years ago when he didn't.

All three admitted under cross-examination that they would not, personally, fly with the pilot while he was engaged in a sex act with an unrestrained passenger.

The fourth witness was the pilot, who defended himself by pointing out that his certificate had been suspended shortly after a flight in Mexico which ended in a wire strike. This seems an odd defence but he argued that the suspension had given him time to think about what he'd done and that he'd already learned his lessons. He said that he made decisions differently now than he had when the incident occurred, a whole four years ago. He stated that he had been rehabilitated during the suspension and intervening three years and now had the qualifications necessary to hold an Airman Certificate and thus he was appealing for his licence to be reinstated.

The law judge did not agree.

> As I said, the conduct that evening was grossly reckless and I'm surprised that the Administrator even put careless in the pleadings because careless shows some sort of negligent act. This was a deliberate act that was reckless clearly on its face.

The judge then reviewed the evidence, which I hope doesn't mean that he watched the video one more time. He stated that the expert witness had proven that the pilot's access to the helicopter controls was at risk and that the video made it clear that both occupants were unrestrained (by which he was referring to their seatbelts, not the style of their lovemaking).

He found that the pilot had violated § 91.13(a) when he performed a sex act with a female passenger while airborne, while both the passenger and respondent had lap belts and shoulder harnesses unlatched, while respondent's clothing during the performance of the sex act risked interfering with the helicopter's controls, and while the passenger was in a position to interfere with the helicopter's controls, all of which occurred as respondent was operating the helicopter above a populated area.

But the pilot wasn't finished yet and filed for appeal. His appeal raised four points:

1. whether the evidence supports the judge's finding that the pilot's conduct during the operation was "gross recklessness"

2. whether the judge improperly admitted medical testimony

3. whether the Sanction Guidance Table provides for revocation in this case (that is, there's no specific mention of sex in the cockpit as interfering with flight safety)

4. whether the respondent lacks the qualifications necessary to hold an Airman Certificate

On appeal, his first point was immediately rejected. There was no real room for manoeuvring here: the evidence was the video which clearly showed that the pilot was engaged in a sex act during the flight. The pilot seemed convinced that the FAA had to establish real danger or that the flight was in peril. However, based on the law, potential endangerment is sufficient.

> Even after conceding the accuracy of the video evidence, respondent appears to focus exclusively on the misguided contention that his access to the aircraft's controls was not restricted, and accordingly, he had no difficulty maintaining control of the aircraft. This assertion, however, seems to ignore the import of key facts in the case: the passenger was leaning across one of the essential aircraft controls, the collective. Her head was occupying a space very near the cyclic control, another critical aircraft control. Her body was unrestrained and vulnerable to G forces, including negative G forces, from any sudden aircraft maneuvers in flight.

The board also brought up the fact that the pilot had unfastened his own lap belt and shoulder harness.

> Respondent's argument that his aircraft was not in danger of hitting the ground or another aircraft, or going out of control, therefore seems to ignore not only the risks he took on the flight in question, but ignores the laws of physics as well.

They also made the point that the pilot had to hold the whole responsibility for the actions in the helicopter during flight.

> Beginning at the point in the videotape before the passengers actually boarded the helicopter, the female passenger exhibited not only an innocence to the ways of flight and the intricacies of helicopter operations by partially disrobing and allowing the respondent to hover the helicopter practically overhead and just feet from her body, but also displayed the typical passenger's willingness to entrust one's safety and well being to the judgment and skill of the pilot.

> Unfortunately, on this flight, that trust was rewarded by respondent's demonstrated careless disregard for the welfare of that female passenger, the camera operator filming the enterprise, and the many, many people in the city below unaware of the reckless behavior

transpiring overhead.

The pilot's second point is arguing the testimony by the FAA witness that:

> ... the respondent would have been distracted or could have incorrectly manipulated the controls of the aircraft in the event of a "biological reaction" to the activities during the flight

It wasn't clear as to why the pilot believed that this testimony was prejudicial. The judge firmly disagreed that the reference to a biological reaction was an improper medical opinion.

> ... we would expect our judges to be able to assess the evidence on videotape and apply judgment, common sense, and their understanding of common events to the circumstances.

I think it's clear what he means by common events. The pilot's third point, regarding the Sanction Guidance Table, was similarly dismissed. If we agree that the pilot acted carelessly or recklessly during the flight, then the Sanction Guidance Table offers revocation as a response.

Beyond this, the board pointed out that the FAA also had grounds for revocation simply based on the pilot's record of sanctions and revocations in the past. Even if the flight in question was dismissed, the FAA could show the past history "demonstrated a lack of willingness or ability to comply with statutory or regulatory requirements" and revoke the certificate based on that alone. He also was charged with reckless operation of an aircraft in 2006 when he landed a helicopter on a public road without a permit, although no disciplinary action resulted. That time was to pick up Motley Crue drummer Tommy Lee to take him to a Nine Inch Nails concert.

The fourth point goes back to the idea that the pilot was "rehabilitated", that enough time had passed since the incident that he had learned his lesson and did not deserve further sanctions.

> ... a significant temporal gap between the conduct and the enforcement action can overcome a lack of qualifications, because a respondent who, at the time of the conduct, might have lacked the qualifications to hold an airman certificate may now possess the requisite care, judgment, and responsibility.

The case that the pilot gave as a precedent had a gap of 17 years between the event and the enforcement action. In this case, the helicopter flight was only four years before the enforcement action. In the meantime, he'd had his licence suspended for operating an un-airworthy helicopter and, during that flight, striking a wire. The pilot argued that in the intervening three years, he had changed.

The summary was pretty scathing:

> Respondent has not convinced this Board that he possesses the care, judgment, and responsibility to hold an

airman certificate, in 2005 or today.

The result was that on the 6th of May 2009, the appeal was denied and the law judge's decision was affirmed, thus the FAA's emergency revocation of the respondent's commercial pilot certificate was affirmed. You can read the full judgement in PDF form on the NTSB website: NTSB Order No. EA-5447[7]. I am almost relieved to see that dockets prior to 1 June 2009 are not stored on the NTSB website so there's no quick reference to the sordid details.

At this stage, the pilot could have made a third appeal, this time to the US District Court or the US Court of Appeals. However, he seemed to have had enough by then and did not pursue a third appeal for the reinstatement of his certificate, bearing in mind a pilot can reapply for a new certificate after the revocation period expires and regain his ratings after written, oral and flight tests. Which is exactly what he did.

He did tell the press that if a passenger presented such an invitation again, he would not take advantage of it. He went on to say that people had been relentless about the incident but he still believed it was a lot safer in that helicopter than on the freeway.

In 2014, the pilot was charged with falsifying his FAA medical certificate in relation to two drunken driving convictions and a fourth revocation proceeding was pending. However, in 2015 he lost control of a Cessna 182 over mountainous terrain

7   https://www.ntsb.gov/legal/alj/OnODocuments/Aviation/5447.PDF

after reporting engine trouble.

> The engine teardown examination revealed a hole in the engine crankcase above the No. 6 connecting rod. The No. 5 connecting rod had fractured and separated from the crankshaft, which caused internal damage to the engine and led to the loss of engine power. The internal components exhibited signs of oil starvation; however, the cause of the oil starvation could not be determined.

The pilot and his passenger were killed in the crash. According to Wired magazine, the young lady from the video is now working in computer sales and is very successful in her new career.

Jumping out of a Plane Isn't Enough of a Thrill?

How much does it take to distract a pilot? Well, in this case, the FAA investigation completely exonerated the pilot; however in the interest of thoroughly exploring the possibilities for Unsafe Sex, it seems worth taking a look at what you can and can't get away with in the front seat of a small plane.

Adults became aware of an explicit video being passed around students at a high school which showed a couple having sex in a small plane and continuing through a skydive. The video was handed over to the police who basically said, um, not sure what we do with this and handed it off to the FAA.

The video was made by an instructor at a skydiving school which offers accelerated free fall training as well as tandem skydives for first-time jumpers. The video featured a part-time instructor at the school taking the receptionist for, um, a ride.

The video was a low-budget project. In the early hours of the morning before the skydiving school opened, the instructor and the receptionist met up with a pilot and a camera man in order to create the footage. The good-looking couple boarded the plane naked and were filmed having sex next to the pilot as the flight began and then continuing with their, um, throes of passion as they jumped out in tandem and soared through the sky. The cameraman jumped after them for long range shots and the instructor appears to have had a camera in his hand to get a close-up view of the receptionist's ecstasy. There is no further footage of the pilot or the safe landing of the plane, which would have been the most interesting bit.

The published video begins with the URL and phone number of the skydiving school overlaid on a photograph of a tandem couple mid-air and the words "Wish you were me?" written on the woman's hand held out for the camera. This photograph was, at the time, the landing page image for the school's website and clearly shows the instructor and the receptionist, although they are wearing quite a bit more clothing in the photo than in the video.

It is not clear where the footage was initially released, other than that the instructor posted the video on his blog, where he announced his availability for porn shoots.

> I am Voodoo, your guide into a world of
> perverted adrenaline and sacreligious [sic]
> behavior. Ready or not, here I cum.

I am a CONTRACT PORNSTAR and
pro skydiver and I am the only Pornstar
Skydiver in the world to actually have sex
while skydiving!!! I live2fly and fly2live.
And yes, I am a true NYMPHOMANIAC!!!
MY GOAL IS TO HAVE MY OWN REALITY
SHOW ON MTV!!!

The top comment on this blog post is from
someone who was not very impressed with his
claim to be "the only Pornstar Skydiver to have
sex while skydiving!!!!"

Sorry to burst your bubble dude, but
we were doing this back in the 70's,
without the tandem harness tho, which
makes it somewhat more difficult to stay
"together", but we weren't porn stars
either so I guess you're right.

It was some time later when staff at a high school
noticed that the students were passing around a
copy and they expressed alarm at the sexual nature
of the clip, sending a copy to the police.

The police didn't have far to look for the
source, as the video began with an advertisement
for the flying school. They contacted the owner
of the skydiving school, who claimed he knew
nothing about this video, despite his skydiving
school being featured as a part of it. He fired
the instructor immediately. In an interview
with the local paper, he said that he hadn't yet
decided whether or not to fire the receptionist.
The instructor (well, ex-instructor at this point)

removed the video from his website immediately.

But with clear frustration, the police admitted that they had no reason to charge the skydiving couple.

All of the participants were consenting adults. The flight took place in the early morning with no witnesses, hence no issue of public nudity. The only thing they could come up with was that the couple were having sex within inches of the pilot. They handed the video to the FAA who agreed to investigate.

A spokesman for the FAA admitted that they had no explicit policy on sexual conduct on private planes. The pilot briefly gives the camera a wave before he starts the engine but there is no direct interaction between the couple and the pilot in the footage. Nevertheless, the FAA justified the investigation stating that "any activity that could distract the pilot while he's flying could be a violation."

The shared employment history of the two jumpers has led some to believe that the whole thing was a publicity stunt; the receptionist has been in over a dozen adult films, although this was only her fourth jump.

The owner of the skydiving school claimed that he had no idea they were planning the porn flick and that the couple had lied to the pilot, saying that they had the OK to do the filming when they didn't. He said that the instructor came up with the stunt in order to get the attention of Howard Stern, an American media personality known for tackling controversial subjects. Radio stations who carried *The Howard Stern Show* were fined $2.5 million for indecent content, so there is a vague logic in sending your indecent content to the show...but it does seem to be an oddly specific accusation.

The receptionist said it was a lie. "Our boss was there. Everything was approved. We did plan it out." When asked about her employment status now, she would not confirm whether she had been fired. She told a reporter, "Call it whatever you want, I'm not working there anymore."

It is hard to believe that the owner hired a self-proclaimed Pornstar Skydiver as an instructor and a blonde 20-year-old adult film actress as a receptionist without any secondary intent. He would like us to believe that they conspired to make a sexdiving video which advertised his skydiving school without his knowledge.

He almost certainly decided to distance himself once he was contacted by the police. However, if he'd stuck to his guns, the police admitted in the end that no crime had been committed.

The FAA agreed. In a statement, they justified their stance:

> [There are] no explicit rules regarding sex in a private aircraft. However, a pilot who allows any activity that could "physically jostle" him or cause him to lose control of the aircraft could be in violation of federal aviation regulations.

They concluded that, in this instance, the pilot and the flight were completely proper, even if the activities of the passengers were somewhat questionable.

There was no comment as to whether the two passengers should have been wearing their seatbelts before the jump.

The owner of the school may have been embarrassed to have been involved in the video but, to his credit, he was happy to speak up in defence of his pilot, who kept his job at the skydiving school.

> No, I wasn't concerned. He was in complete control of the plane at all times. I mean he looked back a couple of times. The same thing he does if there are other skydivers in the plane. He is going to look back, he's going to look around to see what everyone is doing.

The fact that the FAA even bothered to investigate a pilot based on a five-minute video that shows him competently flying his plane is somewhat embarrassing. This is clearly a result of the titillating nature of the video, rather than any real concern for what appears to have been a perfectly safe flight.

I did note that the FAA site, which routinely publishes press releases of their cases, did not make any reference to this particular investigation.

The Pornstar Skydiver website no longer exists. The skydiving school is still in business although the image of the tandem couple has now been replaced with three men offering each other a thumbs up in a very platonic way.

Crop Duster Crashes in Gender Reveal Stunt

ON THE 9TH of July 2019, an Air Tractor AT-602 crashed in Turkey, Texas.

Air Tractors are agricultural aircraft and the AT-602 is a good mid-ranged option for a farmer: a single-seater low-wing tailwheel plane with a range of 600 miles and a 630-gallon chemical hopper for crop-dusting or fertiliser distribution.

An advertisement[8] for the Air Tractor AT-602 promises BIG TIME EFFICIENCY.

> With the AT-602, you can do a thousand acres in the morning, save three loads over a smaller plane, and still have plenty of daylight for more jobs.

This particular AT-602 wasn't carrying chemicals in its hopper and it wasn't helping a

---

8   https://airtractor.com/aircraft/at-602/

farmer with his crops.

No, instead it was carrying pink water.

The pilot was experienced, with a commercial licence and certified as a flight instructor. He had about 14,000 hours flight time with 8,000 on type. He was manoeuvring at low altitude when he dumped the water, dyed pink with food colouring, for what was meant to be a spectacular display.

Someone was going to have a baby and the pink water was her way of saying *It's a girl!* Gender reveal parties appear to be a modern thing, especially popular in the US and Australia. Basically, friends and family are invited to a party where something unexpected in pink or blue demonstrates the apparent genitals of a not-yet-born baby.

Initially, this was a relatively staid affair, where one of the parents would slice a specially made cake to reveal pink for a girl or blue for a boy. Over the past decade, they've become more elaborate, including bashing open a piñata filled with pink or blue candies, setting off smoke bombs with coloured smoke and, in one case, an alligator crunching into a watermelon which had been filled with blue jelly.

As the gender reveal parties get more and more extreme, things have started to go wrong. One couple shot pink fireworks at their party guests. Another couple lost their car when they hosted a gender reveal burnout, placing bags of blue powder under the rear wheels ready to burst. Unfortunately the blue powder ignited and set the tyres on fire.

In a more tragic case, a man used a high-powered rifle to shoot a target, so that it would burst open spraying blue chalk everywhere. The explosion started a wildfire which burned 47,000 acres leading to a fine of $220,000.

And just last month, a 56-year-old woman was killed by a flying piece of shrapnel in a gender-reveal party gone wrong.

Woman killed by shrapnel from 'gender reveal' party explosion in Iowa[9]

They spent Friday and Saturday preparing for the moment, according to law enforcement. The family had welded a homemade stand, which was filled with gunpowder, to a metal base. They drilled a hole for a fuse and placed a piece of wood on top of the metal stand. Colored powder was then layered on top of the wood.

Then, they put tape on top of the entire assembly, which "inadvertently created a pipe bomb," authorities said.

Although I don't quite get the obsession with this kind of embarrassing display, I have to admit that flinging the equivalent of a large hot tub of pink water from a crop-duster seems almost tame in comparison. The pilot slowed and trimmed the aircraft and dumped about

9   https://www.washingtonpost.com/nation/2019/10/28/woman-killed-by-shrapnel-gender-reveal-party-explosion-iowa/

350 gallons (1,325 litres) of water. But then, he said, the AT-602 "got too slow" and then stalled. Already low to the ground, he had no chance to recover and the aircraft crashed into a field and rolled over. His report to the NTSB also stated that his passenger had suffered minor injuries.

Crop duster wreckage

Passenger in a single seater? Sure enough. The report has tick boxes for which seat the passenger was in: left, centre, right. The pilot simply ticked "unknown". The inspector told the NTSB that as far as he could tell, the pilot moved to the right of the seat with the passenger perched on the left edge.

It seems likely that releasing the water that quickly pitched the aircraft violently. With 14,000 hours and 8,000 on type, the pilot was extremely experienced at crop dusting and shouldn't have been caught out. I presume that he didn't normally attempt to release the contents all at once, let alone have a passenger falling into his lap restricting his access to the dump gate handle.

Looking at that plane and knowing they were crushed into that cockpit with no seat belts or restraints, it's amazing that they both walked away.

I Did It for the Karma

There are a lot of reasons why people make bad decisions, but recently it seems like social media has dialled this up to an eleven. It has become increasingly common for people to seek attention through dangerous and reckless behaviour, and pilots are no exception. From crashing a vintage plane for YouTube views to pilots performing incompetent aerobatics, this chapter explores the consequences of putting online fame ahead of safety.

Impromptu Air Show

T HE PILOT IS known as a YouTube sensation with over 100,000 subscribers. He has posted many great videos of himself gliding around the US in his glider, including honest analyses of mistakes he has made. In 2019, he attended the Aeroplanes, Trains, and Automobiles show at Spanish Fork, Utah and was showing off his glider on the ramp.

His glider was a Schleicher ASW-27, a 15-metre sailplane certified in 1997. Designed by Gerhard Waibel, a famous German sailplane designer, the glider has a super-light structure made from a complex composite of carbon, aramid and polyethylene fibre, which allows it to carry a water ballast system to control the wing loadings. The glider flies at 70 km/h (43 mph, 38 knots) with no ballast and full flaps and has a "never exceed speed" of 285 km/h (177 mph or 154 knots).

Many people were excited to meet him and to see his high-performance glider. Then, apparently, the air show management asked if he would do a glider demo flight for the crowd.

He was flattered to have been asked and started thinking about what he could do to show off the abilities of the ASW-27 glider.

> I do loops all the time and I have been known to do a few low passes so why not put them together and show everyone how much energy and potential a glider has with just a few thousand feet to work with! I towed to 3k' above the ground and the video shows the rest. What a random and interesting experience! FYI—the owner's manual for the 27 has a page specifically on how to do proper loops. My entry speed was at 115 knots indicated and I was pulling 3.5 g's. I think I pulled them off well enough. The wings didn't come off. While that was fun and all, I think I will be leaving the airshow stuff to the guys who know what they are doing. Last 2 things: I sure wish the helicopter ride business would have just waited so I could finish the routine without having to worry about hitting them taking off or landing while I was swooping. And yes, I saw the segmented circle and flew over it. Did you even notice it? That would have been super bad hitting its pole at 185 mph!

The YouTuber called it "a random and interesting experience" and described how he did a series of loops and low passes from a 3,000 foot tow. He then uploaded a nine-minute video after the event.

The video had over 200,000 views. At least one of those viewers reported the flight to the FAA.

The FAA was suitably concerned about the idea of an untrained pilot doing aerobatics over a crowd at an air show. The pilot removed the video from YouTube but of course it was much too late.

FAR 91.303 defines aerobatic flight as:

> ... an intentional maneuver involving an abrupt change in an aircraft's attitude, an abnormal attitude, or abnormal acceleration, not necessary for normal flight.

There are a number of regulations around aerobatic flights and air shows in order to reduce the risk both to pilots and those on the ground, including people not attending the air show.

The YouTuber had thought that he was taking the necessary precautions by not flying over the crowd watching the flights but he repeatedly flew low passes near other buildings. He also says that his lowest loop was 1,900 feet above ground level, although from the video, I have to admit it looked a bit lower than that.

The ASW-27 is type certified for "semi-aerobatics" and the manual that the YouTuber mentions does say that some simple aerobatic manoeuvres are permitted, including positive (inside) looping, lazy eights, chandelle and stall turns. The manual also states that it is imperative that aerobatic manoeuvres are only performed by qualified pilots who have received proper training.

The YouTuber had not had any aerobatic training nor any experience with air shows. Obviously he was not an approved air show performer.

He soon learned that approval from the "airboss", as he called the air show management, and precautions based on having read the manual that came with the glider were not enough, even though the glider is type-certified for semi-aerobatics. He put the video back up, saying that the FAA wanted to make an example of him and so by posting the video, he was helping to educate pilots.

He received a seven-month suspension of his licence.

To his credit, he also updated the YouTube description taking full responsibility for breaking regulations and explaining the actions taken against him.

> I hope this will help other pilots to not have to go through what I have over the last ten months.

However, in February 2021, he posted to his YouTube channel again, excited that he had his pilot's licence back. He called the video FAA Suspension Update! and at some point over the 210-day suspension, he decided that the FAA action was unreasonable.

> I fought the good fight spending many thousands of dollars because I really believe the suspension was not justified, but it was a flea fighting an angry gorilla

situation and they smacked me hard.

> What's funny is during the "trial"
> for my airshow, one of the FAA guys
> arguing against me asked why I didn't
> just call the FSBO and ask if I could fly the
> performance. My response was, "Because
> it was on Saturday and you were closed."
> I thought it was really funny but none of
> them laughed.

The FAA aren't really known for their sense of humour.

In the comments of the new video, a fan asked if, now that his licence had been reinstated, he would consider holding a raffle to take one of his YouTube subscribers for a flight.

He responded:

> Great idea! I love to give rides in two seat
> gliders. Something to think about.

This is followed by another commenter pointing out that this, too, would be attracting unwanted FAA attention, with a consideration as to whether he was acting as a pilot-for-hire without a commercial licence. Well, quite.

One thing that bothered me was the lack of any further mention of the air show management and the "airboss". The organisers surely must have known that it was against the law to ask a pilot with no aerobatic experience to put on a display on the day of the air show. Not to mention the fact that, as nothing was rehearsed, the YouTuber appears to have been dodging helicopters during his flight display. I was unable to find any comment on this, although I noticed that the official event video[10] does not show the glider flight and the only comment on the page, asking if any video of the glider flying display existed, has gone unanswered. The event has since been renamed "Wings and Wheels".

10   https://www.youtube.com/watch?v=pj99qDIb-YXQ

All Aircraft Bite Fools

Iт was a few minutes after midnight when the pilot and his friend took the Cessna 150, a popular single-engine two-seater training aircraft, out for a local flight around a general aviation airport now known as the Colorado Air and Space Port.

In 2011, the state of Colorado applied to the Federal Aviation Administration (FAA) to certify the airport as Colorado's first spaceport, although they had no actual plans for suborbital take-off flights. Seven years later, their application was approved, and the spaceport is now waiting for a space company to be licensed as an operator.

However, this late-night flight was in 2014 and so the spaceport, just a few miles from Denver International, was still known as Front Range: a small general aviation airport which acted as the base for a few flying schools and air-rescue training.

The pilot held a commercial pilot certificate

and was qualified as a ground instructor, so it is reasonable to assume that he knew something about flight safety. He was instrument-rated: certified to fly in non-visual conditions using instruments alone. He'd accumulated 99 hours in simulated environments and 14.7 hours actually flying in instrument conditions. In the two months before the accident, he'd logged 27 hours night-flying and half an hour in simulated instrument conditions.

It is unclear whether he had kept up with the minimum requirements to fly in instrument conditions or to take passengers.

On the 30th of May at 23:59, the weather at Denver International Airport was calm, with mist reducing the visibility to two and a half miles (approx 5km) and clouds at 300 feet. Half an hour later, another weather observation showed scattered clouds as low as 200 feet.

Night flying can be under visual flight rules if the pilot has a clear view of the ground However, the low cloud cover that night meant that any flights would be under "night instrument meteorological conditions". The pilot must focus on the instruments because it isn't possible to orient oneself by looking out at the ground and the horizon. Flying with instruments is not instinctive but requires focus and concentration, especially for someone with only a hundred hour's instrument experience, most of which was simulated.

That night, the pilot only planned a short local area flight and so he had no need to file a flight plan or to talk to air traffic control.

It wasn't until 3:30 that someone noticed that the

aircraft was missing. After the sun came up, Front Range Airport personnel discovered the crumpled wreckage in a wheat field near the airport.

Twisted wreckage of the C-150

Radar returns showed that the Cessna 150 had departed normally just past midnight. They followed the traffic pattern around in a standard circuit. This means that after take-off, the pilot keeps making 90° turns to create a sort of rectangle while keeping the runway in sight (crosswind, downwind, base and final), until the aircraft is in the correct position to land on the same runway that it took off from. This is what the Cessna did: climbing to a height of 900 feet above ground level and then following the pattern back to final. It landed just a few minutes after take-off.

Ten minutes later, they departed again. This time, the Cessna seemed to drift to the left as they climbed away at rate of about 300 feet per minute. The pilot turned right, towards the northwest. As they reached about 640 feet, still climbing, the pilot started a left turn. They had gained only another hundred feet when the left turn began to tighten into a steep bank. Suddenly, the Cessna started descending at 1,900 feet per minute. The radar lost sight of the aircraft at 140 feet above the ground.

The left wing struck the ground first. The crashing aircraft created a small crater in the field before bouncing back into the air, coming down hard a short distance further.

The pilot was thrown clear of the aircraft; the passenger was slumped in the remains of the cockpit. Both of the occupants were killed on impact.

The right wing had detached from the aircraft and was found lying on top of the crumpled left wing. Glass and pieces of aircraft fuselage were scattered between the crater and the wreckage. The emergency locator beacon had not activated but was still armed and attached to the antenna.

Despite the violence of the crash, the main controls of the aircraft, the elevators and rudder and ailerons, were still connected and moved freely. The flaps were retracted and the trim was set to neutral, as one would expect. The fuel tanks had plenty of fuel.

In the centre of the crater was a slash mark from the propeller, which showed that the engine was still running when it struck the ground.

Nothing was mechanically wrong with the aircraft that hadn't happened in the crash.

The first responders found a GoPro camera in the wreckage, miraculously still in one piece.

The data card was unharmed. The footage did not include the accident flight but it did include seven other clips that appeared to have been taken the day before and the day of the accident. The GoPro had been mounted to the instrument panel area in front of the pilot. It faced backwards to capture the faces of the pilot and the front-seat passenger and a partial view outside the left and right windows.

Although the accident flight was not included, these video clips told their own story. Even though they had been filmed earlier, they were included in the final report as evidence of the pilot's operational habits.

In the first video, which seemed to have been taken the day before, the pilot and a passenger entered the aircraft and adjusted their seatbelts. The pilot looked at his phone and then reached back to grab a notepad before ending the recording.

In the second video, we see the pilot and the same passenger as the Cessna taxis to the runway. The pilot runs through his power checks as he follows the taxiway and he then speaks to air traffic control. The video ends before they reach the runway.

The third video starts at the take-off roll, with the pilot and the same passenger onboard. The Cessna 150 takes off and the pilot follows the traffic pattern for a single circuit, the same as he had done the night of the accident. As he flies, he lifts his smartphone to take a few photographs of himself. He clearly takes a selfie on the base leg and seems to take another during the final approach. The passenger also takes photographs of the flight and himself. The GoPro footage ends as the aircraft clears the runway.

The fourth video, probably taken the day of the accident, shows a new passenger in the cockpit with the pilot. The aircraft follows the taxiway but, this time, the pilot does not appear to do his power checks. The Cessna enters the runway and takes off. The passenger has his hands on the controls, following the pilot's movements, but does not appear to be actively manipulating the controls. Then the pilot makes a series of abrupt movements on the controls, entertaining the passenger by putting them briefly into negative-G. The pilot takes a few selfies and then they land and taxi back to the hangar area. The passenger gets out to let a new passenger into the cockpit, the third passenger to appear on the videos. Passenger 3 takes multiple selfies as they taxi to the runway. The pilot checks the automatic weather recording for the airport but does not appear to use a checklist or to do any pre-flight checks. The passenger holds up his phone to record out the front as they start the take-off run. As the aircraft takes off, the pilot reaches to move the passenger's phone out of the way, as it is blocking his line of sight. Then, as they climb away, the pilot gets his own phone out and begins taking selfies. The passenger also takes a few selfies and the video ends as the aircraft turns crosswind.

The fifth video appears to be during the same flight. They are still in the air as the pilot interacts with his phone. Then he reached for the control yoke for some mild negative-G moments. After landing, they return to the hangar area while the passenger takes more selfies. The previous two passengers walk out to the hangar area to greet the pilot and the passenger, who disembarks. They all take photographs of each other and the plane. A fourth passenger enters the aircraft as the video ends.

The sixth video shows the pilot and the new passenger taxiing to the runway and then taking off. As the aircraft climbs away from the runway, the pilot looks at his phone and taps at it. He turns crosswind and then interacts with the phone again. They turn downwind and the pilot rocks the wings while the passenger takes selfies. Then the pilot lands the plane. He returns to the hangar area and shuts down the engine.

These videos repeatedly show a dangerous lack of attention to the aircraft. The pilot is regularly distracted from his surroundings while he took selfies and interacted with his phone during critical phases of flight. Even on final approach, just seconds before landing, he seems to be more interested in his phone than in the plane.

I would not automatically assume from this that he would be equally inattentive on a night flight such as the accident flight. Except that on the final clip retrieved from the GoPro, taken that same evening, the pilot goes back to taking selfies.

When the footage starts, the pilot is in the cockpit with a new passenger, his fifth passenger over the course of the GoPro filming. The rest of the group is in the shot, standing behind the aircraft. The pilot starts the engine and listens to the automatic weather information, which announces that the weather is calm and overcast at three hundred feet, the same weather as was forecast for the fatal crash.

The pilot follows the taxiway to the runway, checking the controls for freedom of movement. They enter the runway and the pilot applies power for take-off. The Cessna has just lifted off from the runway when the pilot holds up his phone and points it at himself. The cockpit area fills with the light of the flash and then goes dark again. The pilot then interacts with the camera app on the phone, seemingly to look at the photographs or perhaps the camera settings.

They land but, while the Cessna is still travelling to a halt on the runway, the pilot looks down to interact with the phone again. The recording ends.

After seeing this footage, it is not hard to conclude what happened that night. At night, above the cloud cover, all they could see was the dark and the mist and the cloud. Distracted by taking photographs of himself and blinded by the flash, the pilot could not help but become disoriented. With no horizon or view of the ground, he couldn't quickly make sense of his position. The turn became steeper and steeper until they flew straight into the ground.

There's an old saying in aviation: All aircraft bite fools. I guess we need a modern corollary: no plane waits for the fool and his selfie.

Barrel Rolls for TikTok

THIS MIGHT DESTROY my street cred, but I'm not going to lie: I loved Top Gun: Maverick. Yes, it is effectively military fan fiction. Yes, it was odd that they kept talking about "there's a 5th generation fighter out there" to make sure that they never gave a hint as to who the enemy was. Yes, it was silly and over-the-top, and yes, it was relentlessly sentimental. Even so.

But sometimes the desire to sing along and be a part of something so very Hollywood isn't good. The excitement about the new Top Gun movie led to a video appearing on TikTok which quickly went viral.

The video shows a young woman posing in front of a red Cirrus SR-22. Kenny Loggins' "Danger Zone" begins to play.

The Cirrus SR-22 is one of a line of light aircraft that have picked up the nickname "Doctor Killer", as a very expensive high-performance aircraft used for personal aviation. It's also known as "the plane with the parachute," as it has a whole-plane emergency recovery parachute system that can be released in flight. The aircraft was launched in 2001 and by 2014, almost a hundred and fifty American registered SR-22s had crashed, with 122 fatalities. Percentage-wise, the overall accident record is better than average for light aircraft but the number of fatalities is high. Better training, especially training for using the parachute system, started bringing the fatality rate down. It is not certified for aerobatic operations.

The video shows the view from over the wing as the aircraft takes off. The same young woman, now belted in and with a headset on, smiles excitedly. She turns her camera to show the landscape outside. It is a beautiful day with blue skies and not a cloud in the sky. The words "wait for it ." appear overlaid on the blue screen and then the horizon begins to tilt. Soon, the landscape drops out of view and we can see nothing but the blue, blue sky. A pair of sunglasses floats past. Finally, we see the ground at the top of the window as the aircraft flies upside down. She pans the cabin, showing herself and another passenger with phone out in the back and two young men in the front as the pilot continues the roll and straightens out. The video then cuts to another flight, this time with her sitting in the front right seat. She gives a thumbs up to the camera and shows a young man sprawled on the back seat, eyes closed. "Sleeping = I had to scare my friend :rofl:" appears over the sleeping man as the aircraft banks hard to the left. The man throws his hands in the air as he is flung to the side. The woman laughs happily.

The next caption, white against a dark sky, says "Barrel Roll". Then the city lights come into view as the aircraft turns upside down.

This clip of the aerobatics at night was originally posted to her Instagram without the Top Gun music in 2019. "We're going to do a barrel roll," she says and then screams in delight as if on a roller coaster.

It isn't clear from the video exactly what manoeuvre the pilot is trying to do but what he ended up with was definitely not a barrel roll. It seems like he might have been attempting to fly an aileron roll and then slipped to the side as he tried to bring the wings back straight and level.

The ailerons are a hinged section on the back of the wing; when the pilot moves the yoke or the stick in the cockpit to turn, this changes the position of the ailerons on both wings. If you moved the control column to the right, the right-wing aileron would move up while the left-wing aileron would move down. This changes the lift so that the aircraft rolls to the right, entering a hopefully gentle turn. If you continue, you would enter a steep turn of 60°.

For an aileron roll, the pilot applies full aileron in one direction, rolling the aircraft until the wings are vertical. If the aircraft is travelling fast enough, then the airspeed will, for a short time, keep the aircraft flying despite the lack of lift. The pilot continues the roll while applying rudder in the direction of the bank as the aircraft turns upside down and then rolls back to straight and level.

A barrel roll, originally known as a "side

somersault", is a combination of a loop and a roll. The name comes from the fact while the aircraft is rotating both longitudinally and laterally, the result looks like it is corkscrewing through a barrel.

The most famous barrel roll is almost certainly when the test pilot Tex Johnston rolled the prototype for the Boeing 707 while demonstrating the aircraft to VIP representatives from the Aircraft Industries Association. You can watch the video on YouTube by searching on Boeing 707 Barrel Roll—Pilot Tex Johnston[11]. Now, Alvin Melvin "Tex" Johnston was a remarkable pilot. He was a test pilot for Boeing and he was intimately acquainted with exactly what the aircraft could do.

If you imagine a plane flying straight at you while turning, that's an aileron roll.

An aileron roll, if properly executed, should only exert a very light positive g-force. The Cirrus SR22, however, is not even rated for a turn with an angle of bank that exceeds 60° (a standard steep turn).

So, let's make a list:

- Passengers on board an aerobatic flight must wear a parachute.

- It wasn't a barrel roll; it looks like it was meant to be an aileron roll (but he screwed it up).

- Thus, the pilot is not trained for aerobatics.

- The SR22 is not approved for any aerobatic

---

11   https://www.youtube.com/watch?v=AaA7kP-fC5Hk

manoeuvres.

- Aerobatics are illegal over populated areas.

The poster has clarified that she was only a passenger and never in control of the aircraft and it may have been her who misidentified the manoeuvre. We don't know what the pilot actually aspired to as we have only the passenger's description. But either way, the manoeuvre was not executed correctly, starting from the passengers not belted in and not wearing parachutes (although, to be fair, at least the aircraft was wearing one) to the floating sunglasses to the clear slipping at the end of the roll.

It seems very much like the pilot was attempting to teach himself aerobatics in a plane not rated for aerobatics, with passengers on board, at night.

A Certified Flight Instructor who watched the video commented:

> The actual certification is not that
> important. People do aerobatics in normal
> category aircraft, but these people are
> often better than the average pilot.
> The problem is most people consider
> themselves better than the average pilot,
> yet few actually are.

An Aviation Safety Inspector (GA Ops) also commented on the video but with a simple image: an emoji of a detective with a magnifying glass.

Meanwhile, on TikTok, the passenger who

posted the video complained that commenters were "wanting to take the fun out of everything." A number of people tried to explain to her exactly how chilling the video was, as opposed to just a bit of fun. She pinned a comment to the post.

> This video was from a random invite
> from over 3 years ago. I'm not the pilot.
> I've never been a pilot. I had no clue how
> dangerous this was.

Since then, the viral video and the comments have all disappeared.

Although there are sure to be copies of it, that video was itself a compilation of older videos. The pilot was only shown in flashes as the passenger panned her phone around. It seems unlikely that there will be any action.

The only saving grace of her compilation is that the SR22 is distinctive enough that the video may dissuade other TikTokers from accepting an invitation to a pleasure flight with that pilot.

Many people like to put down social media video sites such as TikTok and YouTube, but I strongly suspect the FAA love them for making their job so much easier.

Social Media Influencers Weigh Down Aircraft

THE FATAL CRASH at Scottsdale Arizona took place directly after take-off. The passengers were a self-proclaimed crowd of social media influencers. The jet-setting influencer who had organised the flight had an audience of 12,000 followers who followed his exciting lifestyle on Instagram. He had been dating the same woman for six months. "It was a big deal," his roommate said to Fox News. His friends were even more famous. He had invited another avid traveller who, according to his brother, enjoyed being an influencer on Instagram where he had almost 44,000 followers. A further passenger was a pretty blonde who had left high school to become a model, with 28,000 followers for her Instagram: glamour shots of lounging by the pool under the hashtag BikiniLife. Her last post was a video of the aircraft with the all-caps caption OFF TO VEGAS.

The aircraft was a Piper Comanche, a single-engine light propeller plane which usually has four seats but can be extended to six, as this one had. The Comanche was owned by a company which was run and managed by a single person. A second company held a one/sixth share of the first company and thus, indirectly, of the aircraft. There were two shareholders in the second company, both pilots. One of them, a professional airline pilot, had only flown the Comanche once. He had planned to use it for his private transportation, but then decided that the travel benefits he received through his work meant that he didn't need access to the small plane.

He was friends with the jet-setting Instagrammer and sold him his share in the partnership and helped him to organise flight instructions in the Comanche so he could learn to fly.

The jet-setting Instagrammer took a few lessons from his flight instructor, although it's not clear how many hours of instruction he had received. He had not yet organised his medical certificate, which is required before students can be authorised for the first solo.

He had flown in the Comanche with his new partner in the shareholding company a fortnight before the crash. It was a warm day with four people on board and a hundred pounds of luggage. The partner said that under the circumstances he was surprised by how well the Comanche performed, maintaining a climb rate of 700 feet per minute.

The Instagrammer told his friend, the one from

whom he'd bought a share of the aircraft, that he wanted to fly a group of friends from Scottsdale, Arizona to Las Vegas, Nevada, but his flight instructor had backed out of the flight. The friend put him in touch with a qualified pilot who could take the role of Pilot In Command for the flight.

This qualified pilot agreed to pick up the Comanche in Las Vegas and fly to Scottsdale, where he would pick up the jet-setting Instagrammer and his friends and fly them back to Scottsdale. However, he said, this could not be considered an instructional flight, as he hadn't done any ground work with the student.

That evening, the friend got concerned when the Instagrammer told him that the Comanche was full of fuel and that there would be six people in total on board. He asked the student about the total weight.

A pilot should calculate the weight and balance for every flight. You start with the empty weight of the aircraft, in this case, 2,007 pounds. Then you total the weight that you are adding: the people on board and any cargo, of course, as well as the total weight of the fuel. You may not need full fuel for the flight, for example, so with a full aircraft, you may wish to save weight by only filling the tanks halfway.

You add all of the weights to find the gross weight. You also need to work out the "total moment" which you use to work out your centre of gravity (CG): effectively, the point that your aircraft balances on. This point will move forward or backward depending on how the aircraft is loaded.

If the centre of gravity is outside of the acceptable range then the aircraft's lift and performance is affected. For example, if the centre of gravity is too far back (aft), then the nose will be high. This can cause the aircraft to lift off from the runway early, before the aircraft has enough speed to fly. This is why the weight and balance must always be checked that it is within the safe envelope for operating the aircraft.

The truth is that in general aviation people often take shortcuts. Having worked out the weight and balance for a specific configuration, they often will do a quick calculation based on approximate weights. There's always a risk involved, however, and one should be relatively confident about what the aircraft can take and where it needs to be placed in order to do this.

The friend sent a text message: "Make sure you guys aren't over weight or anything. [Pilot] is by the book."

Instagrammer: How do I do that?

Friend: Do you have five people going?

Instagrammer: 3 small girls 2 medium guys. 6 total.

Friend: What about luggage?

Instagrammer: Small stuff that's light and will be on their laps.

It's noticeable that the Instagrammer owns shares in the aircraft and is confident enough to organise the trip but does not have any real idea about the weight and balance of the aircraft.

Friend: What's the max gross weight of that plane?

Instagrammer: 1,200.

The max gross weight of the aircraft is 3,200 pounds, but neither the Instagrammer nor the friend seemed to realise that 1,200 didn't make sense.

Friend: Yeah, you're good. Just go over it with [Pilot] when you add fuel.

Spoiler: he was not actually good.

Now, to be fair, I would expect the qualified pilot, who has agreed to fly the plane, to insist on checking the weight and balance. Apparently he was not quite as "by the book" as the friend thought he was, however, because he appears to have simply taken the Instagrammer's word for the fact that the aircraft could handle six passengers with some luggage on full fuel. The Comanche is actually designed as a four-seater and, although it can take six passengers, the pilot will need to be strict on luggage and avoid filling the tanks full of fuel. The friend, in fact, has assumed that the Instagrammer and the pilot will take this into consideration when they add fuel. He had clearly missed or forgotten that the Instagrammer told him that the tanks were already full.

Meanwhile, the Instagrammer appeared to have been reassured by this conversation that he'd done his due diligence and all was well.

That day, our qualified pilot arrived at North Las

Vegas Airport to pick up the Comanche. It was the first time the company manager had met him and he knew nothing about the planned night flight. He said later that he considered not letting him take the aircraft. The qualified pilot explained that he had been hired to pick up the Instagrammer in Scottsdale and bring him back to Las Vegas.

The manager was already nervous about the flight without knowing that the fully fuelled plane was going to pick up another five people. But as far he knew, the pilot was only picking up the Instagrammer and to be fair, the Instagrammer was taking lessons and had a share in the aircraft. The manager checked that the pilot had the relevant experience, including 200 hours flying the same type of aircraft, and decided to let him take the Comanche.

Back in Scottsdale, the group travelled to the airport. A man working at the front desk of a company offering general aviation services said that about quarter past eight, a tattooed man came in from the street to ask if this was Signature FBO. The man explained that it was not and gave instructions to get to Signature FBO, another company offering services at Scottsdale. Then he phoned Signature to tell them that they might wish to send a car over, as some of their customers were in the wrong place.

The tattooed man was the Instagrammer. He left and came back a short while later accompanied by three women and another man. He told the man at the front desk that he'd spoken to the pilot and told him where to pick them up, so they no longer needed to go to Signature.

Then the group sat down at a table in the main lobby and spread out take-away food that they had brought with them. The man at the front desk said that they were well-mannered and in good spirits, not commenting on the fact that they were not actually customers and had simply parked themselves in his lobby.

He heard the Instagrammer tell the others that he was learning to fly and soon would be able to fly solo. One of the group then came to the desk to ask where the aircraft was.

The man knew nothing about the flight and couldn't find any details about the inbound aircraft. However, it wasn't long before the qualified pilot arrived. The group finished their meal and walked out to the ramp to board their aircraft. The man looked out and saw the Comanche. He said later that he was surprised to realise that the entire group was planning to fly in the small plane. The pilot walked into the lobby and appeared flustered but didn't speak to anyone.

The group took photographs and videos of the aircraft and uploaded them to social media sites, bragging about the flight to come. The Instagrammer took the front left seat, traditionally the seat of the Pilot in Command, and the qualified pilot took the right-hand seat. Now to be fair, this is a typical seating arrangement for a student and instructor, even though it is the instructor who is considered the Pilot in Command of the flight. But we should remember that this was not meant to be an instructional flight and the qualified pilot should not have been ceding any control to the

Instagrammer. Although the Instagrammer owned a share in the aircraft and had taken a few lessons, he was in no way experienced enough to make any decisions about the Comanche. The qualified pilot had not instructed him and he alone, as Pilot in Command, carried the responsibility for the aircraft and the flight.

A woman working the ramp noticed that it took a few tries to start the engine, which was odd as it was still warmed up from the inbound flight. She asked a co-worker if that was normal but didn't receive a response. The engine started on the next try and she watched the Comanche taxi to the runway, noticing that all of the passengers were staring at their phones.

The Air Traffic Controller in the tower saw the lights of the Comanche as it turned onto the runway.

The woman on the ramp heard the sounds of the power check and then the Comanche came back into view as it started its take-off roll. It looked to her like the aircraft was rolling from left to right. She then saw the nose begin to pitch up and down and she wondered if the pilot was playing around.

In the dark, the tower controller could only see the aircraft lights but he also noticed that the wing lights were moving up and down, as if the pilot was rocking his wings. By the time the Comanche passed the tower, the wings appeared stable but he noticed that the engine didn't sound like it was producing enough power.

He contacted the flight and asked if they were experiencing any difficulty. A confident call came back, saying "We're good. We're just in training mode."

The Instagrammer's friend who had helped to arrange the flight said that the voice sounded like that of the qualified pilot; however, he couldn't understand why he would refer to it as a training flight.

An airport operations technician who was setting up barricades had the tower radio playing through the overhead speakers. He heard the controller ask someone if they were experiencing any difficulty. He glanced at the runway and saw the Comanche coming towards him. He too noticed that the engine didn't sound right.

> The engine sounded as if it was not completely at full power as other planes have sounded before. I was not sure if it was struggling or if it was just that particular type of engine. It did not sputter or sound rough, nor were there visible smoke, fire or vapors. It was just producing a low tone as if it had lower RPMs.

The controller, the woman on the ramp and the technician all watched with concern. The oscillations seemed to have stopped as the Comanche began to pull away. It seemed to be struggling to climb and continued straight. The Comanche was about two hundred feet above the ground, the height of the buildings around it, when it began turning to the left. The woman on the ramp saw the nose drop as the aircraft disappeared from her sight. The man at the end of the runway said that the left turn started before the end of the runway, much earlier than a normal departure. He saw the Comanche continue turning and start to descend.

A man and his wife were driving past the airport when they saw the Comanche. "Look how low that plane is flying," he said to his wife, who was driving. He kept turning to watch, horrified as he realised that the aircraft was turning too steeply to recover.

A traffic camera recorded the scene. The aircraft was in a left bank and the bank angle increased as the aircraft descended. The wings were almost vertical when the Comanche crashed into the ground and exploded into a fireball.

The couple in the car called 911 (US emergency services) who said that the control tower had already been in touch. The couple drove to the crash site in case they could do something, but it was immediately clear that no one could have survived.

The aircraft had smashed into the ground. The seats had detached and one passenger was thrown clear of the wreckage. The right-wing and auxiliary fuel tank were wrapped around the base of the tree. The left wing fragmented and the fuel exploded.

The two men were belted in but the four in the back had not fastened their seatbelts. This implies there was no safety briefing. At every point, it seems clear that none of the passengers had any idea what they were getting into.

The autopsy on the student included positive toxicology tests for MDMA (ecstasy) and cocaine at low concentration, indicating use in the past few days, although not considered relevant to the crash.

The investigation found a fracture in the engine which would have reduced the available engine power. The fracture surfaces were fatigued; the break was not new. The reduction in power had not been noticed in previous flights but now that the aircraft was full, it became critical.

The maximum gross weight for the Comanche was 3,200 pounds. As the plane itself weighed 2,007 pounds, the pilot could carry an additional load of up to 1,193 pounds. However, the weights of the passengers and the fuel totalled 3,335 pounds, putting them 135 pounds above the aircraft's maximum gross weight.

The CG range for the Comanche was 80.5 to 93.0 inches aft of datum, an imaginary vertical plane or line from which measurements are taken, established by the manufacturer. The actual CG was 95.22 inches aft, which led to the aircraft pulling away from the runway before it had gathered enough speed to fly.

The result was an overloaded aircraft which was overbalanced to the rear, lumbering up into the air, unable to gather any more of the speed required for safe flight. With a fully functioning engine, a good pilot might have been able to correct for this by maintaining level flight at full power. However, they did not have the additional power they needed to pull this off. As they started the left turn, the aircraft fell out of the sky like a brick.

A friend of the Instagrammer said, "I am sad that he is gone, but loved how he lived life to the fullest." If a full life involves attempting to defy the rules of physics for a photo-op, then I guess I'm going to give it a pass.

Vintage Plane Crash for You-Tube

IN THE COURSE of aviation history, there have been a multitude of bad decisions leading to the destruction of a plane, but this is perhaps the only example of a pilot abandoning his aircraft to crash into the mountains, all for the sake of YouTube views.

It seems somehow worse that it was a vintage plane which is no longer in production and cannot be replaced. The Taylorcraft B is a single-engine high-wing monoplane designed by CG Taylor as direct competition to the Piper Cub, which was also designed by CG Taylor. Taylor had founded a company called Taylor Brothers Aircraft Corporation in 1926, later Taylor Aircraft, which struggled with financial issues during the Great Depression. William Piper, known as "an oilman", bought the company for a paltry $761, keeping Taylor as the company president.

Within five years, Piper ousted Taylor from the company and changed the name to the Piper Aircraft Corporation. CG Taylor decided to start his own aircraft company in direct competition with Piper: the Taylorcraft Aircraft Company. The B was their second model and the naming convention of BL-65 becomes obvious when you consider its Lycoming 65 horsepower engine.

The owner of this beautiful aircraft was an Olympic snowboarder who churned out YouTube videos of his adventures, including flying, skydiving, freight train hopping and more. With over 133,000 subscribers, the pressure was on to keep designing adrenaline-fuelled content. He had newly purchased the single-engine plane and installed cameras inside and out for multi-angle footage.

On the day of the accident, he set off from Lompoc Airport in California for a flight to Mammoth Yosemite Airport. Smiling at the cockpit camera, he explained that the flight was planned as a memorial for his late friend, who had entered the public eye at seventeen, as the youngest person ever to climb the "Seven Summits". Unfortunately, the friend was killed at just 23 years old, during the filming of a wingsuit video that he'd described as "very dangerous" when he called a California radio station to tell them about the event.

The Taylorcraft was in good shape and the departure and initial cruise were uneventful. The pilot smiled as he held up a baggie of ashes in front of the cockpit camera and explained that he was going to spread them over the mountains.

But during the flight to Mammoth, the aircraft suddenly lost engine power. The pilot was wearing a parachute and holding a handheld camera mounted on a selfie stick, he leapt out of the cockpit and landed with only minor injuries. The unmanned aircraft descended quite a bit faster than the skydiving pilot and crashed in Los Padres National Forest, suffering fatal injuries—sorry, "substantial damage".

A few weeks later, the video appeared on YouTube titled "I Crashed My Airplane". It quickly became his most popular video with over a million views over the course of the next few months. Although the YouTuber is no longer uploading new videos, his edited version of the plane crash is still on YouTube[12], neatly tidied up to remove the worst of the incongruities and any reference to the flight having had a commercial sponsor. As of this writing, the new version of the video has 2.4 million views.

The video begins with a beautiful and clear California day at Lompoc Airport. The pilot waves a small plastic bag at the cockpit camera. In the original video (since removed and replaced), he smiles at the camera and explains that these are the ashes of his friend which he plans to scatter at Mammoth Mountain. Coincidentally, I happen to know that in the state of California, you cannot scatter human ashes over land without the written permission of the landowner. In the case of State Parks, this permission would be granted by the Park Superintendent, who

---

12   https://www.youtube.com/watch?v=vbYszL-NZxhM

will make sure that the scattering is not over lakes, streams or sites which hold the remains of Native Americans. I never thought I'd need that information twice but I'm just saying, you can't simply take a sandwich bag of someone's ashes and throw the ashes around Mammoth.

At any rate, at about fifty-eight seconds into the video, the engine cuts out. Although there are multiple camera angles, none of the footage offers any view of the instruments or the controls, so it is very difficult to know what the situation is other than the propeller has stopped. The pilot pulls back on the yoke, slowing the aircraft down. He doesn't try to restart the engine or find out what might be wrong. Instead, he pushes open the cockpit door, which appears to already be unlatched, and looks at the ground below. He also never considers the possibility of a forced landing. In the original version of the video he explains, "There was no safe space to land."

Flat areas and a riverbed are clearly visible on the video, easily within range of his gliding aircraft. An anonymous pilot familiar with the area posted this Google Maps link to the accident location and points out that the valley east of the Manzana Schoolhouse Camp would be an obvious area for an emergency landing but it is not visible from the careful framing of the pilot's video. The anonymous pilot also states that there are multiple flat areas (meadow and fields) within five miles of the aircraft at the point when the engine failed.

Completely coincidentally, he is wearing a skydiving parachute and has a selfie stick close to hand, ready for his jump. As the pilot exits the cockpit, the aircraft can be seen descending as the propeller begins to windmill.

As he falls through the air, he twists to keep the Taylorcraft in sight. The parachute expands and the aircraft glides below him and over a lovely dry flat riverbed. He turns to float towards it.

The pilot watches as the Taylorcraft crashes into the hills, and then he comes down in rough ground nearby, calling out "oh my god" over and over. He scans the area with his camera, saying that there was simply nowhere to land here. "Where the hell am I going to land a freaking plane? I'm going to die. That's why I always freaking fly with a parachute."

I have often been asked if I wore a parachute while flying the Piper Saratoga. I did not, because quite frankly, if I could get the aircraft stable enough to open the cockpit door and climb out for a safe jump, then I could almost certainly attempt a landing. The pilot explains in the video that he always wears a parachute while flying; however the parachute he pulls out is not the type of parachute that test pilots and military pilots wear. In addition, as many have pointed out, a quick scan through his other videos shows that he does not "always" wear a parachute, but in fact seems to have put it on especially for this video.

As he walks through the bush, he complains that he has cuts everywhere and a few bruises from the impact and complains that there is poison oak, everywhere. If he'd brought the Taylorcraft down for a rough landing, he could have avoided this.

He struggles through the brush to make it to the

wreckage of his plane, showing us the crumpled wings. Then he hikes across the wilderness until sunset, when he is forced to stop for fear of falling and injuring himself worse. At some point shortly after that, he hears a car and manages to flag down farmers passing by on a dirt road.

The video ends with him in his paragliding equipment, distributing his friend's ashes and saying goodbye. The edited version of the video now available is about four minutes shorter, missing key details such as the explanation at the start that he is posting this video so that other pilots could learn from his experience.

The pilot reported the accident to the National Transportation Safety Board (NTSB) and the Federal Aviation Agency (FAA). Normally, the NTSB would not investigate a straight-forward engine failure such as this one, however, a preliminary report was released in January 2022 under the accident number WPR22LA049 and the status is marked as "in work". As of March 2023, the investigation is still in progress and the docket has not been released.

Apparently, the pilot and a friend chartered an aircraft to remove the aircraft from the site. The NTSB preliminary report states that no representative travelled to the scene, so presumably they knew no evidence was to be found there.

Video sites have a number of recreations of the flight in Microsoft Flight Simulator. My favourite was by a local pilot who used the simulator to fly to the area and pulled the throttle to idle at the same location, flying at the same altitude. Not only were there a number of opportunities for a forced landing but the pilot was able to glide the aircraft to an airport and land safely on the runway.

A set of three screengrabs have been posted on Reddit which appear to show that the pilot had a fire extinguisher strapped to his leg under his trousers, which is certainly not where any pilot would think to keep an extinguisher as protection against an onboard fire.

The FAA were somewhat quicker to react. They opened their investigation on the 29th of November, before the pilot had even posted the video on his YouTube channel. It's not clear what alerted them. Sources at the Lompoc airport told the press that the aircraft was in need of major maintenance; however, the pilot did only minor fixes on his own before the fated flight. He appears to have prioritised the installation of all of the cameras over ensuring that the aircraft was airworthy.

On the 1st of April, 2022, the FAA released an emergency order of revocation. Their summary of the event is that the pilot jumped out of the Taylorcraft wearing a sport parachute backpack container, causing the plane to crash into the Los Padres National Forest.

"I did not crash my plane for views," claimed the pilot. However, the FAA disagreed, bringing the following points:

1. Prior to this flight, you attached multiple cameras to the outside of N29508, including a camera pointed in the direction of the propeller, in order to record video footage of the outside and inside of the

plane during the flight.

2. Prior to this flight you put on a sport parachute backpack container.

3. During this flight, you opened the left side pilot door before you claimed the engine has failed.

4. Prior to jumping out of the aircraft you made no attempt to contact Air Traffic Control on the emergency frequency.

5. Prior to jumping out of [the aircraft], you made no attempt to restart the engine by increasing airflow over the propeller.

6. Prior to jumping out of [the aircraft], you made no attempt to look for areas to land safely, even though there were multiple areas within gliding range in which you could have made a safe landing.

7. You jumped out of [the aircraft] while holding a camera attached to a selfie stick and continued to record the aircraft during your descent.

8. After the crash, you recovered and then disposed of the wreckage of [the aircraft].

9. After the crash, you recovered the cameras that you had attached to [the aircraft] prior to this flight.

10. The conclusion: Your flight on November 24, 2021...was careless or reckless so as to endanger the life or property of another. Federal Aviation Regulations specify that

no person may operate an aircraft in a careless or reckless manner so as to endanger the life or property of another.

The FAA used this regulation to pull the pilot's Private Pilot Certificate and any other airman certificates issued to the (now ex-)pilot, for the safety of aviation and the public.

> Your egregious and intentional actions
> on these dates indicate that you presently
> lack the degree of care, judgment and
> responsibility required of a certificate holder.

Now the truth is, the pilot can apply for a new pilot's licence in a year. However, one can hope that he would be asked to demonstrate that he has learned better judgement and a sense of responsibility. In addition, the State of California and the Department of Transportation could also seek judgement against him. Meanwhile, the NTSB investigation of the event is still in progress. In what I would consider a win for the public interest, the YouTube channel is now dormant, with no new videos uploaded since the FAA action.

The NTSB report is not meant to apportion blame but to consider how such an accident could have been avoided. It will be interesting to see what they come up with.

In Case of a Water Landing

Crashing into water doesn't make for a soft landing. In this section, we explore the dangers of ditching, from malfunctioning seaplanes to a self-driving jet.

Reckless River Flying

THIS CASE FROM New South Wales is a particular tragedy as the pilot's reckless flying led to the death of a passenger in the aircraft, a young girl who was travelling with her father.

On the morning of the 12th of April 2014, the pilot arrived at Casino Airport. He was well-rested and had no medical issues that might have affected his operation of the aircraft. His medical certificate had expired but when he was examined a few weeks later, there was no issue with a renewal.

He wore polarised sunglasses, unaware that both Australian and US aviation authorities do not recommend polarised lenses when flying. Although they reduce reflected glare from horizontal surfaces, they can also mask the "sparkle" of light reflecting off shiny surfaces.

His aircraft was a Maule M-5, popularly known as the Lunar Rocket. It's an American four-seater high-wing aircraft. Maules are very recognisable modern tailwheel planes. They are referred to as taildraggers because they are designed with a tailwheel instead of a nose wheel. Taildraggers are popular as bush planes: low maintenance aircraft that can take off and land on short runways. The Maule taildraggers are especially popular in Alaska and Canada, as they can take off and climb quickly in awkward circumstances with a fair amount of weight in the back. The Maule's short-field capabilities have been described as legendary.

The pilot kept the Maule M-5 in a hangar at Casino Airport and went flying several times a month.

That morning, the pilot completed his pre-flight inspection as normal: all was well with the plane. He then flew to Lismore airport to refuel.

He planned to fly to Bonshaw, about 175 kilometres west of Casino, to visit a family member. He invited a work colleague to accompany him, arranging to pick him up at Murwillumbah and they would fly to Bonshaw together. At the last minute, they arranged for the colleague's 11-year-old daughter to join them on the pleasure flight.

They departed Murwillumbah in good spirits. The pilot sat in the front-left seat, as normal for the Pilot in Command, and his colleague sat in the front right seat. The daughter sat in one of the rear passenger seats. The pilot helped her to adjust and fasten her seat belt through the rear cabin door, which is on the right of the aircraft. The pilot and front passenger seats had three-point seat belts with lap and shoulder restraints. The rear seats only had lap belts; at the time when the Maule M-5 was manufactured, shoulder restraints weren't required for rear passenger seats, although they are installed as standard on newer models.

The work colleague said later that he doesn't remember the pilot briefing them about seat belts and safety issues, although he said that he understood that they were expected to keep the seat belts fastened throughout the flight.

The three of them departed Murwillumbah to the southwest shortly after 09:00. Once en route, the pilot changed his mind about continuing to fly to Bonshaw, as they encountered strong headwinds and a lowering cloud base over the mountains. They landed at Tenterfield Aerodrome and the pilot discussed the change of plan with his passengers.

He decided they should track back east towards Ballina, and he could take them to look at the Clarence River along the way.

The weather improved. As they arrived at the Clarence River, the pilot descended to between 800 and 1,000 feet above the ground. He tracked south towards a section of the river that he was familiar with, an area that he thought was called "The Cascades". He scanned for power lines as he flew, spotting one which had been marked with high visibility markers.

They were just north of Baryulgil when he recognised the area he was looking for. He turned north and descended to tree-top height to follow the river back the way they had come. By now, only broken clouds were in the sky and visibility was good. The pilot said that there was only a slight ripple on the water from the wind and the flying conditions were generally smooth. His recollection is that he was flying along the river at about 100 knots (185 km/h).

An eyewitness who was about 5 kilometres north of the Cascades on the western bank of the river saw the aircraft. It was sometime between 10:30 and 11:00. The witness noticed that the aircraft appeared to be flying at "normal speed" but very low. This would have been noticeable as an aircraft in normal flight must keep to a minimum specified height unless there are unavoidable reasons to fly lower or if the aircraft and pilot are approved for specific low-flying operations (for example search and rescue).

From the ATSB report:

> Specialised training and endorsements are required to conduct approved low-flying operations. This training includes the relevant operating techniques and procedures to safely operate in a low-level environment, the procedures to follow prior to descending to commence low-flying operations, and identifying the types of ground-based infrastructure frequently associated with hazards such as powerlines. This includes power poles and the cleared easement that often exists in the immediate vicinity of a powerline.

In fact, the ATSB have collected data on the numerous low-flying accidents which they have investigated, of which a significant number both involved wire strikes and proved fatal to the pilot and/or passengers. Of these, many were the result of unauthorised and unnecessary low-flying, where there was no operational reason for the pilot to be flying so close to the ground. They released what I'm sure is a riveting publication entitled *Avoidable Accidents No. 1— Low-level flying* in 2010, which discusses seven accidents, of which only one had survivors. The second in the series, *Avoidable Accidents No. 2— Wirestrikes involving known wires: a manageable aerial agricultural hazard*[13], deals specifically with strategies developed to help agricultural pilots manage the ongoing risk of wire strikes during spraying operations. And I know you'll be thrilled to hear that there's another half dozen in the series, although the rest don't deal with low flying. My favourite title is Starved and exhausted: Fuel management aviation accidents.

In Australia, the aircraft must be 1,000 feet above any city or populous area and 500 feet over the terrain or obstacles on that terrain in any other area.

They had no reason to be flying this low: the equivalent of driving along the pavement to look into shop windows.

The pilot did not hold a low-flying approval and he had not received any low flying training. In this case, he should have been flying at least 500 feet *above* the trees, not at "tree-top height".

They continued to track the river heading north.

They encountered a sharp westerly bend and the pilot pulled up, climbing to about 400-500 feet above the ground. Then he made a spur-of-

---

13   https://www.atsb.gov.au/publications/2011/
avoidable-2-ar-2011-028

the-moment decision to descend back down to tree-top height and fly further north along the river, although this included a section of the river that he wasn't familiar with. After the bend in the river, the west bank of the river was slightly higher than the eastern bank.

As he descended back to tree-top height, still banking left to follow the bend in the river, the pilot saw wires immediately ahead.

Two power poles, one on each side of the river, held two galvanized steel cables, each containing three wound strands of 2.75mm diameter wire, spanning 665 metres across the river. They carried 11kV of electricity.

There was no warning. Why would there be? There was no aerodrome in the area and no expectation of low flying. The Australian standard only recommends the permanent marking for overhead cables that exceed a height of 90 metres (295 feet).

But these cables were only 16 metres (53 feet) above the waterline on the eastern bank and 25 metres (82 feet) on the western bank. They were too low to require permanent marking as there was no reason why an aircraft would be at risk of flying into them.

The cables themselves were only about 6mm (¼") in diameter and had become weathered and dull grey.

Can you see the cables?

By the time the pilot saw them, it was much too late.

The left wing of the Maule M-5 struck the wires at two different points. The cables cut through the structure of the wing's outboard leading edge, the mid-section leading edge and the wing support strut.

The cables did not break, although the power poles were damaged and a significant amount of cable was dislodged from the poles. A high-voltage protection device about three kilometres away detected a fault as it happened and isolated the power.

As the first cable struck the left wing, taking out a big chunk of it, the nose yawed violently. The second cable then struck the leading edge of the same wing, taking another chunk from it. The pilot lost control and the aircraft crashed into the river. The windscreen shattered. The right wing folded rear wards, blocking the cabin door.

As the aircraft impacted the water upside-down, the water flooded the cabin. Still reeling from the impact, the occupants needed to escape.

The aircraft came to rest upside-down, a short distance from the power lines. The cockpit was inverted, fully submerged and flooded.

The pilot was bruised across his left shoulder and both hips from the three-point seat belt. His passenger in the front seat had been seriously injured in the initial impact. Both had chemical burns from the aviation fuel that had poured out of the wings.

The pilot managed to release his seatbelt and escaped from the cockpit through the forward-left cockpit door. The front-seat passenger also pulled himself free through the forward-right cockpit door. The pilot struggled to open the rear cabin door to free the passenger but it was impossible to open. He eventually managed to drag her out of the plane through a cockpit door.

The pilot and her father were unable to resuscitate her. It was much too late: she had broken her neck as they crashed and died as the aircraft was still flooding.

The pilot trekked to a nearby property to find help. It took hours for emergency services to make it through to the accident site. The front-seat passenger was winched to an ambulance helicopter and flown to Lismore Base Hospital. The pilot was taken by ambulance.

The Northern Star wrote about the incident:

After a painstaking operation lasting all
day, the plane was finally dragged from
its resting place and towed upstream
to a waiting truck at about 5 pm. The
job started about 10 am from Yates
Crossing—a shallow causeway about 3
km upstream—where a flat-bottomed
SES boat borrowed from Lismore was
launched into the Clarence to venture
downstream to the crash site.

If he had been trained in low-level flying,
the pilot might have noticed the power-line
easement through the nearby scrub, or the power
poles close to each river bank.

But he wasn't trained and he did not know
the hazards or techniques for flying close to the
ground. Despite this, he thought it was a good
idea to make what the ATSB called a spur of the
moment decision to fly along an unfamiliar
section of a river at very low level.

The pilot of the aircraft was charged with
manslaughter, recklessly inflicting grievous
bodily harm and endangering the life of another
by flying below 500 feet. Two years after the
accident, he was sentenced to a 15-month
suspended jail sentence for reckless flying. The
front-seat passenger, the girl's father, said in court
that he wished that he had died with her that day.

Fatal Seaplane Crash at Oshkosh

Pᴉʟᴏᴛꜱ ᴀʀᴇ ᴏꜰᴛᴇɴ the lightning rod when things go wrong, an easy scapegoat. This is because they are often the very last safety net, which means that a final small error in a long chain of bad management can be fatal, making their failure an easy target for us to point at. Blaming the pilot makes for a simple solution to a complex problem; after all, if the pilot can be retrained or is no longer flying, then we can consider the problem solved. This allows more complicated problems to be swept under the carpet. An ongoing temptation, because issues such as bad design, training deficiencies, operational issues and poor maintenance are much more difficult to deal with. It's handy to have someone to blame and that is why we need to be careful not to be too quick to point fingers.

However, there are some accidents where it is possible for the entire sequence to be laid at the feet of the pilot. This fatal crash in 2017 is one such case, a tragic crash which would have been avoided if the pilot had been willing to slow down and listen.

He was extremely experienced: he held an airline transport pilot certificate with 33,467 flight hours, rated for single- and multi-engine land and single-engine sea planes. He had been an FAA pilot examiner for over 46 years and had certified nearly 3,000 pilots. In 2013, he was inducted into the Minnesota Aviation Hall of Fame. This makes it all the more difficult to understand what went wrong that day.

He was the owner and sole pilot of the accident aircraft, an Aerofab Inc. Lake LA-4-250 Renegade amphibious aircraft built in 1983, registration N1400P. The six-seater Lake Renegade set half a dozen new records for single-engine amphibians in the late 1980s, including world records for altitude, sustained flight and sustained flight at altitude. The founders of Lake Amphibious Seaplanes, with strong ties and experience in the aerospace industry, claimed to have developed the only single-engine boat-hulled amphibian in production in the world. The company has been up for sale since 2009, having last manufactured an aircraft in 2007. However, the Lake Renegade aircraft are still popular as amphibian aircraft in the US, including the military version of this model known as the Seawolf.

EAA AirVenture Oshkosh is an annual fly-in convention organised by the Experimental Aircraft Association (EAA) and held every summer in Oshkosh, Wisconsin, a small town on the banks of Lake Winnebago. In 2017, it ran for ten days, from the 21st to the 30th of July. AirVenture is one of the top events for the aviation community in the US and, afterwards, the Chairman said the event had been incredible.

> From the U.S. Navy Blue Angels and Apollo reunion, to new aviation innovations on display and two B-29s flying formation as part of 75 years of bombers on parade, it was a week filled with only-at-Oshkosh moments. You could feel the energy as thousands of airplanes arrived early and stayed longer, pushing aircraft camping to capacity for most of the event. The aviators and enthusiasts who attended were engaged, eager, and passionate, demonstrating how Oshkosh is the best example of why general aviation is so vitally important to the country. I believe it's the best AirVenture week that I've ever seen.

That week, over 10,000 aircraft flew in for the event and Wittman Regional Airport, the centre of the event, had 17,223 aircraft operations over the ten-day event, averaging 123 take-offs and landings per hour. The other airports hosting the event include Pioneer Airport for helicopters and airships, Ultralight Fun Fly Zone for ultralights, homebuilt rotorcraft and hot air balloons and Vette/Blust Seaplane Base on Lake Winnebago for seaplanes.

It was not quite so incredible for the surviving family and friends of the three occupants of the

Lake Renegade.

On the 27th of July 2017, the pilot decided to fly to Vette/Blust Seaplane Base to attend AirVenture with two passengers. One of the passengers was a flight instructor with 3,000 hours flight time, with 1,600 hours instruction and 150 hours on type. He said that he had trained the pilot for seaplane flights and had personally conducted about a hundred water landings in Lake Renegade aircraft. The other passenger did not have any piloting experience.

The weather that day was clear with heavy swells at Lake Winnebago. The Lake Renegade landed in a bay south of the sea base and began to taxi north along the shore towards Seaplane Base. After a few minutes, the pilot contacted the base to say that they were taking in water and needed help.

Everyone in the area mobilised to help, with five boats and ten volunteers quickly making it to the scene. The harbour master followed in his tow boat and saw the left wing was low in the water and heavy. When the chairman of Seaplane Base arrived, he saw the aircraft drifting towards shore, just 30 feet from the rocky shoreline. First, the volunteers manoeuvred the aircraft away from the rocks. Then a tow boat positioned itself to the right of the Lake Renegade. A passenger in the tow boat had to hold down the right wing in order to prevent the left wing from dipping into the lake. Like this, they were able to tow the aircraft into Seaplane Base.

The left wing sponson, a buoyancy casing that extends from the hull like a short wing in order to increase stability on water, had been taking on water since the seaplane had landed. They dragged the left sponson onto the dock, where the pilot removed a plug and drained a large amount of water. Then the harbour master pulled the aircraft to a mooring plug to park.

The pilot and his two passengers left and returned about two hours later. A volunteer helping with AirVenture took the pilot to his mooring.

The volunteer boatman said that the pilot boarded the Lake Renegade. He watched as the pilot started the engine without untying the mooring plug first. The aircraft began to turn in a circle, tethered to the buoy. The boatman stopped the pilot, asking what he was trying to do.

The pilot was belligerent. "You can't prevent me from leaving with my aircraft!"

The boatman patiently explained that he was just trying to help and that the pilot was not going to be able to leave unless they untied the aircraft from the buoy. Once the Lake Renegade was untied, the pilot told the volunteer to tow him to the ramp, so that he could drain the left sponson.

At the ramp, he asked for a water pump. Staff there asked him why and worriedly wondered if he had water in the aircraft hull. The pilot said no, he did not, and proceeded to drain the water out of the sponson manually. Then he opened the drain valve for the fuel tank in the left sponson and began draining the fuel...directly into the water. The harbour master grabbed a bucket and asked the pilot to please drain the fuel into it. At the same time, some of the personnel at Vette/Blust Seaplane Base noticed that underneath the left wing, outboard of the sponson, an inspection cover was missing.

The pilot drained the left sponson fuel tank until it ran dry, about four to five gallons of fuel. Then he closed the drain and said that he was leaving the base.

The conditions at Lake Winnebago had deteriorated in the time that the pilot and his passengers were at Oshkosh. By now, the waves were 18 to 24 inches high (around half a metre). The staff explained that the water conditions were too rough for the seaplane. They were right: the Lake Renegade is considered safe for a maximum wave height of 18 inches. Three pilot briefers all attempted to convince the pilot that flying out now would be unsafe in the heavy waves.

The pilot insisted that he wanted to leave, regardless of the conditions. The briefers called the chairman of Seaplane Base and asked him to intervene.

The chairman told the pilot that they were concerned about his planned departure because of the rough waves. He convinced him to come out on a boat and they would check the weather and water conditions in the outer bay. As they motored to the outer bay, the pilot agreed that the waves were too big and that the conditions were unacceptable.

But then, to the chairman's surprise, the pilot said that he was still leaving, he would simply take off parallel to the swells.

The chairman pointed out that this would mean a downwind take-off, instead of taking off into the wind to increase take-off performance.

Then he lost his patience. "You will NEVER get airborne with a Lake, with full fuel, three passengers, heavy wave conditions and downwind—NEVER!"

The pilot disagreed. For one, he said that he wouldn't be taking off downwind, saying that the wind was clearly blowing from the northwest. As they returned to the protected bay of the Seaplane base, the chairman pointed out that every aircraft was pointing into the wind, showing that the wind was coming from south-south-east.

At the dock, various members of the Seaplane base tried to talk him out of flying, explaining that they were just trying to help him. The pilot simply told them to take him back to his aircraft.

Once back at the base, the chairman tracked down another Lake Renegade pilot, who immediately agreed that the water conditions were too rough for take-off and told the pilot so. They also offered to help the pilot to find lodging for the night.

He refused, insisting that he was going to load his passengers and depart.

One of the sea base staff reminded the pilot of the missing inspection cover underneath the left wing, without which the aircraft was not airworthy. The harbour master towed the aircraft to a repair dock where they found a scrap piece of aluminium which the pilot duct taped to the hole as a temporary field repair. The harbour master recalled that the aircraft sat normally in the water, with no sign that the left sponson was still taking on water. He towed the aircraft from the dock to "the cut", a narrow gap leading from the base to the bay. The pilot said he was going to start the engine and the harbour master held up one finger to signal that he should wait until he'd towed them into the bay. The pilot repeatedly asked to start his engine; each time, the harbourmaster asked him to wait.

After the accident, the pilot's friend and flight instructor, who was the only survivor of the crash, said that, as far as he knew, the pilot had gone to the dock and received a briefing from the staff. Then, the pilot had gone out with the staff for a visual look at the water conditions and decided that they were good for departure. The instructor never had any idea that the pilot had been warned that conditions were unsafe and that the briefers had literally pleaded with him not to go.

At the outer bay, the moment that the harbour master disconnected the tow ropes, the pilot started the engine. He immediately applied full power for take-off.

The chairman watched the aircraft start its take-off run with a 90° crosswind. About halfway through the take-off run, the pilot changed direction, until they were heading northwest with a direct tailwind. Then he realised that the flaps were still up: the aircraft was not configured for take-off.

The Lake Renegade continued to accelerate and then began to bounce, "porpoising" across the high waves.

This is a common issue with seaplanes. A Lake flight instructor told investigators, after the fact, that a water take-off with a two-foot sea state (waves at 24 inches or 60 cm) should only be attempted by a very experienced pilot. He taught his students to retard the throttle immediately during a water take-off if they felt the thump of the fuselage making contact with the water, and then pause, allowing the aircraft to settle. More experienced pilots, he said, might not retard the throttle immediately, but might allow for two or even three thumps while porpoising.

The pilot did not retard the throttle. After the third thump, the nose rose steeply out of the water and then rolled over to the left. The left wing caught the waves, spinning the aircraft by 180°. The nose dipped into the water and started to sink.

The engine remained at full power until it had sunk into the lake.

A witness told local media[14], "We saw the plane come out of the seaplane base, and it looked like it was having some trouble getting up. We were saying, 'Come on little plane you can do it!' Then all of a sudden we realized it had just gone down."

The Lake Renegade came to rest in about 15 feet of water with the right wing partially buried in the mud. Everyone in the area rushed to the scene to help the occupants. As the first responders drew close, a man pulled himself out of the aircraft and inflated his life jacket. It was the flight instructor; the pilot and the passenger were still inside.

The harbour master dove into the water and forced open the left cabin door, where he found the pilot, slumped and not responding.

14   https://fox11online.com/news/local/fox-cities/eaa-seaplane-hit-wave-before-it-went-down-in-lake-winnebago

Someone passed the man a knife which he used to cut the pilot free of the seatbelt. He pulled the unconscious man to the response boat. As they administered CPR, the harbour master returned to the wreck, where divers were attempting to release the passenger from the back seat. It took two of them to pull her free and they pulled her to the response boat where CPR was administered. Both were taken to hospital in critical condition. The passenger and the pilot both died in hospital in the days following the accident.

Investigators from the NTSB recovered the Lake Renegade wreckage a few days later.

> Both left and right wing spars exhibited buckling. The right wingtip was bent upward into the right aileron and the fuselage exhibited buckling deformation immediately forward of the empennage. Continuity was verified between all control surfaces and the cockpit flight controls. The landing gear handle was in the UP position and the landing gear were found retracted. The flap lever was found in the UP position and the flaps were retracted.

> No preimpact anomalies were noted that would have prevented normal operation of the airplane or engine.

So nothing was wrong with the seaplane. Toxicology tests were negative for tested-for substances, excluding the possible influence of drugs or alcohol on the pilot.

The flight instructor, the only survivor of the flight, had a relatively clear recollection of the chain of events. The pilot started a powered-up circling take-off in the bay. The plane broke water, he said, and then hit some waves. From his seat, it seemed that after bouncing about three times, the right sponson caught a wave and sucked it down, at which point the plane flipped on its side with the right wing on the water. The right door popped open on impact but by then he was underwater and it was difficult to push the door open against the water rushing in. Once he got out of the aircraft, he said he looked through the left-side window and saw an air cavity in the cockpit but, shortly after he escaped, the plane sank.

He was sure that the pilot had performed the preflight checklist before taking off. He also said that he remembered the pilot calling out that the flaps were down (set for take-off) as a part of the checklist.

However, the witnesses at the dock were very sure that the flaps were not down for the take-off, as they had commented on this directly. An examination of the wreckage showed that the flap selector lever was in the UP position.

Later in his statement, the flight instructor claimed that in the Lake Renegade, the flaps did not have to be extended for take-off.

This is not true. The Airplane Flight Manual (AFM) for the Lake L-250 clearly states that flaps are used for *all* takeoffs and landings. Step 14 of the *Before Takeoff* checklist is to verify that the wing flaps are down. In the cockpit, a printed checklist was clipped to the instrument panel which also included the clear requirement to verify that flaps were set DOWN for take-off and landing.

Checklist in the cockpit

Did the flight instructor, who said that he had trained the pilot for seaplane flight, also teach the pilot that flaps were not necessary? Based on his statement, it is not clear whether the pilot forgot to set the flaps for take-off, simply reading off the word "down" out of habit as he rushed through the checklist, or if he intentionally did not set them in hopes that it would help him with the tailwind take-off over the swells.

The NTSB summarised the sequence of events:[15]

> ...the circumstances of the accident are consistent with the pilot rushing to depart and failing to ensure the airplane was properly configured with flaps extended before taking off. Additionally, the pilot elected to take off with unfavorable water and wind conditions despite the advice from other pilots that he not do so. The pilot's decision to takeoff with unfavorable water conditions and a tailwind, combined with his failure to lower the flaps for takeoff, likely contributed to the airplane stalling as soon as it became airborne and resulted in a loss of control.

In other words, the pilot never had enough airspeed or angle of attack to take off. He attempted to force the aircraft out of the water by pulling back on the controls, causing the wing to stall.

Probable Cause

- The National Transportation Safety Board determines the probable cause(s) of this accident to be:

- _____ The pilot's failure to properly

15   https://data.ntsb.gov/carol-repgen/api/Aviation/ReportMain/GenerateNewestReport/95685/pdf

configure the airplane for takeoff
and his decision to takeoff with
a tailwind in unfavorable water
conditions, which resulted in the
airplane entering an aerodynamic
stall and the pilot losing control.

The pilot's decision to risk a tailwind take-off in an aircraft that had been taking on water a few hours before proved to be his undoing. He dismissed the warnings of the staff and volunteers who begged him not to fly in such conditions, too eager—or too inexperienced at lake flying to understand the rough conditions. In his rush to leave, he either forgot or chose not to configure the aircraft correctly for takeoff. It is very difficult to interpret his actions as anything other than reckless. This recklessness cost him his life, and serves as a stark reminder of why caution and a willingness to delay are so important when it comes to aviation.

How To Drown a Jet

T HIS INCIDENT FIRST came to my attention when a video went viral on YouTube. The video begins with a shaky view of a runway and the sky above, while a voice says, "We've got a nutball, trying to land."

The Cessna Citation 2, registered as OY-JET, had departed Burlington, Vermont with three passengers on board for a business flight to Atlantic City, New Jersey. "OY-" is the registration prefix for Denmark.

The pilot had attached a photocopy of the Atlantic City Municipal Airport/Bader Field (AIY) chart to his control column which gave the airport details. The chart also clearly said, under Airport Notes: "Arpt CLOSED to jet traffic".

Bader Field has been serving Atlantic City since 1910, with an early passenger service starting in 1911. Surrounded on three sides by water, it was able to offer facilities for both seaplanes and land-based aircraft. A newspaper article referred to Bader Field as a "municipal air-port" in April 1918, the first time that the term *airport* had been used. In 1990, commercial travel shifted to Atlantic City International Airport and its 10,000 foot runway. The control tower at Bader Field was removed and part of the land was developed into a minor-league baseball stadium. The airport was closed in 2006.

However, this was the 15th of May in 2005, a year earlier. Bader Airport was still seeing a surprising amount of general aviation traffic.

While the flight was inbound, the pilot spoke to Atlantic City Approach and even said that he was inbound to "alpha charlie yankee". ACY is Atlantic City International Airport. It's 9 miles northwest of Bader Field and has two runways, one of which is 6,144 feet and the other, 10,000. It would have been an altogether better choice for landing the Citation 2.

However, the flight continued to Bader Field and the controller cleared OY-JET for a visual approach at Bader airport.

The pilot flew a low pass over runway 29 and he says he looked at the windsock before climbing out to the right. The windsock is specifically there for a quick visual reference, as it clearly shows which direction the wind is coming from and how hard it is blowing.

By preference, aircraft and ducks always land against the wind, which offers a higher airspeed in comparison to the speed over the ground. This saves energy and allows for a safer transition from air to ground. You can watch this effect for yourself at any airport or duck pond.

On that day, the windsock showed that the

wind was perfectly aligned for a landing on runway 29.

An employee at the airport was manning the radio from a trailer about halfway along the runway. He was speaking to a single-engine aircraft which was downwind for landing on runway 29. Then he looked out the window and saw the Cessna Citation 2, OY-JET climb away from a visual pass over runway 29. It is standard to state your intentions over the radio at an uncontrolled airport, but OY-JET did not make any calls. The employee watched as the aircraft lined up for an approach on runway 11, that is, coming at the same piece of asphalt but from the opposite direction.

Tailwind operations have a number of detriments. During approach, the tailwind will increase the ground speed, requiring a faster rate of descent, which can easily result in an unstable approach. The ground speed will be higher than usual at the point of touchdown and the tendency for the aircraft to float just above the runway will be increased. The increased ground speed and long landing make for a longer stopping distance. This effect is greatest on light aircraft as the tailwind is able to increase the ground speed quite dramatically. Aircraft manufacturers set a tailwind component limit for take-off and landing, which is listed in the Aircraft Flight Manual. For the Cessna Citation, it is ten knots.

The windsock is visible in the video, which shows the wind at about 10 to 15 knots along runway 29. An aircraft normally always lands into the wind. Occasionally, an airport will prefer a runway despite the tailwind for noise abatement reasons but this is strictly controlled and only up to a tailwind component of five knots. Even this can cause difficulty for a light aircraft but, in such cases, there is usually more than enough runway to make up for the longer landing distance needed.

There are times when a pilot may choose to land on what is called an "out-of-wind" runway, but it is relatively rare and certainly not with the wind at over ten knots, which it is on the video. On that day, the out-of-wind runway was runway 11.

The Cessna Citation 2 circled the airfield and came in for a landing on runway 11. It was this that captured the attention of the people on the ground, leading one to film the inbound aircraft.

It's hard to make out much of anything on the video with the camera shaking. The voice says, "I don't know if you can see this." The Citation 2 comes into focus about a third of the way along the runway. It touches down and passes the camera at high speed, continuing along the runway out of sight. Several witnesses said they saw smoke from the aircraft tyres as it attempted to slow down.

"I think he made it," says the voice on the video, full of surprise. He zooms in to the far end of the runway while another voice says, "That guy is one crazy sumbitch."

The Cessna 525A Landing Distance Chart shows that the aircraft with a landing weight of 11,400 pounds would require 3,000 feet of landing distance with no wind. On a runway with a ten-knot tailwind, the Citation 2 would need over 3,500 feet of landing distance.

As noted on the chart, Atlantic City Municipal

Airport/Bader Field (AIY) is normally closed to jet traffic. The full length of runway 11 is 2,948 feet. *If* there had been no wind and *if* he'd landed perfectly and *if* he'd braked the length of the runway, he *possibly* could have stopped right at the end of the runway.

There wasn't enough runway and the airport didn't accept jets and, on top of all that, he landed in the wrong direction.

The pilot still thought it was reasonable when interviewed after the fact. "Everything seemed normal," he said later. "Braking action, speedbrake and full flaps for landing. Good touchdown (even a little hard) and braking action OK."

He didn't mention that he'd touched down around 1,000 feet beyond the approach end of runway 11, leaving him a landing distance of 2,000 feet. "Everything was very normal until two-thirds down the runway … Braking action was totally lost as OY-JET proceeded down the runway."

Actually, treadmarks could be seen about two-thirds down the runway and continuing to the end. The pilot claimed that he "lost the brakes"; however, once the aircraft was recovered, no fault was found with the brake system or the emergency brake system.

The pilot didn't attempt to explain why he ever thought he could land on runway 11 in the first place.

The aircraft is out of sight in the video but the voice cuts in. "You're kidding me! Holy shit." The video jiggles and bounces, showing only asphalt as the person starts running. It then cuts to the view out of the front of a car or van, windshield wipers running, while the voice fills us in. "All right, he went off the end of the runway and we dialled 911. It was obvious he was going downwind when he landed."

Although the aircraft had seemed to slow at the end of the runway, it did not stop and went straight over the edge and into the water.

The video shows the plane floating in the water. A small boat has pulled up to the wing and the occupants of the Citation are climbing out onto the wing and into the boat. The overfull boat rocks and a second boat appears to help take the people back to safety. The wail of sirens can be heard in the background. "I think everybody's OK," says the voice, zooming in on the boats at the nose of the floating Citation. "They redefined the word gambling in Atlantic City on that one."

As the smaller boat drifts along the side of the boat towards the nacelle, a high-pitched whine can be heard. "Oh shit," says the voice. "The engine is now running, I think." Steam appears around the tail, obscuring the OY-JET registration and the people on the boat stand up and begin to shout.

"They are cutting the rope," says the voice, while another one pipes up in the background, "They left the engines still running, I can't believe it." Under normal circumstances, the pilot should have cut off the fuel and the power, which would ensure that the engines couldn't relight. That said, no one expected the aircraft to start back up again while half under water. The voice starts to sound panicked. "Get away, get away!"

The boat leans precariously as they try to get away from the aircraft as the engines spool up, the tail lifting out of the water. The boats quickly motor away, seconds before water begins to spray out of the engine. "Oh boy," says the voice. "The jet is now powering forward." The aircraft moves slowly, water spraying chaotically behind it. Motor boats appear briefly in the background as they circle the Citation from a safe distance. "Maybe he'll taxi back up on land," says the voice, dubiously.

The pilot was visible on the boat in the earlier footage, although the voice couldn't have known that. Apparently a short circuit caused the engines to relight. There's no one in the cockpit, which becomes clear as the nose pitches steeply up. The Citation turns in a full circle before the engine eventually stalls out and the video ends.

The pilot's statement to the NTSB starts with "In my 2000 Hrs or more as a single pilot and more than 350 Hrs on this type, a Cessna Citation has never brought me and my passengers that close to what happened in Atlantic City." He ends with "To me, it appears that the braking system is not designed well to handle the CJ2 aircraft at different weights and software parameters may limit the braking action (deceleration) or cause inconsistent braking action."

He had no comment as to why he was landing on a runway which did not have sufficient length for a normal landing or how it was that he landed with the wind behind him, adding another 500 feet to his required landing distance.

The NTSB have published Probable Cause[16]:

> The pilot's improper decision to plan a
> flight to a runway of insufficient length,
> his improper in-flight decision to land on
> that inadequate runway with a tailwind,
> and his failure to obtain the proper
> touchdown point.

Other than that, though, it was a lovely landing. Bader Field was closed in 2006, a year after this incident. The land has been sitting up for sale for years; however, in 2022, Philadelphia YIMBY[17] reported the details of a three-billion-US-dollar plan to redevelop the airfield site as an upmarket neighbourhood featuring canals inspired by Amsterdam and Venice.

The owner of the Cessna Citation 2 showed a great sense of humour about the incident. The ruined aircraft was replaced with a Cessna 680. The new registration? OY-WET.

---

16   https://data.ntsb.gov/carol-repgen/api/Aviation/ReportMain/GenerateNewestReport/61495/pdf
17   https://phillyyimby.com/2022/11/3-billion-development-plan-unveiled-for-atlantic-citys-bader-field.html

On a Wing and a Prayer

T HIS ACCIDENT took place on the 3rd of July 2021 on Lake Michigan, but the real story starts eight days before that.

The aircraft was a Seawind 3000, a fixed wing single-engine amphibious aircraft. The defining event is listed as *ditching,* which seems odd for an amphibious aircraft which regularly lands on water. The poor little Seawind 3000, still at the bottom of Lake Michigan, might not feel that it fulfilled the criterion of "a controlled landing".

The pilot was on the last leg of an eight-day cross-country trip from Bracket Field in California to Traverse City in Michigan when the engine sputtered and then gave out completely, and a burning smell wafted through the cockpit. The pilot attempted an emergency landing on Lake Michigan, which was almost successful, despite the fact that he wasn't able to extend the flaps or retract the landing gear. The pilot was rescued from the wing shortly before the aircraft sank.

The pilot had purchased the Seawind 3000 just over a week before the accident. The pilot was alone in the aircraft and he was rescued before the aircraft sank, so that's a pretty good outcome. In fact, it is an amazing outcome considering the situation.

The NTSB report is only one page long. When queried if the aircraft was going to be recovered, the FAA representative in Grand Rapids was rather dismissive.

> Sorry, I do not have [the pilot's] email. I have attached a time line for this mess and there is no intention to locate or salvage the aircraft off of the lake floor. Let me know if you need anything else.

The timeline that he refers to is a nine-page statement by the pilot which completely overshadows the NTSB report.

The operator of an aircraft is required to notify the NTSB after any accident. This statement usually includes the type and registration of the aircraft, the name of the owner and the operator of the aircraft, the name of the Pilot in Command, the date and time of the accident, the last point of departure and point of intended landing, the number of persons aboard and the nature of the accident.

This pilot submitted a statement entitled *Returning to Flying*. It might be the most beautiful docket document that I have ever read.

I have edited it slightly for clarity. Please note that this is the pilot's version of events; if we spoke to the original owner, things might look a bit different.

It starts with an explanation.

> After twenty years, my sons had their lives and families budding and I wondered about flying again. When my boys were very young, we built an experimental aircraft. Lancair Super ES: all fiberglass with a 350 hp motor which seated four and took to flight after 22 months of building in the cabinet shop, which was located in Billings, Montana, flying to Bend, Oregon for the annual fly-in for Lancairs (over the Rockies of 14,000 feet). Deciding to be close to family in Florida, I sold the house we and my boys' mother designed, the cabinet shop 5,000 foot building, auctioned the tools and took our first leg to Omaha, Nebraska. Spending the night there, we continued all the way to West Palm Beach, FL, the following day arriving at sunset.

These recollections continue, filling the first page of the report until the author finally gets to the point, which is that in March 2021, he decided to purchase a Seawind 3000. The Seawind 3000 is a kit plane designed in Canada; in 1999 the standard kit retailed for $59,000 with an estimated $50,000 of additional components necessary to assemble the aircraft. The company estimated it would take the average builder 2,000 hours to construct the aircraft.

This particular Seawind 3000 had been put together in 2008. According to the pilot, the owner supplied photographs and an information packet which showed the aircraft to be in pristine condition with a spotless engine. The for-sale price was listed as $185,000.

The pilot paid a deposit of $1,000 to reserve the aircraft. Over the next few months, while he waited for his house to sell, he paid an additional $3,000 to the owner in order to ensure that the aircraft was not sold to another customer. His house sold in June and the pilot paid the remainder. Then he flew to California to pick up the aircraft. There he planned to fly with the seller for a few days to learn how to operate the Seawind. Then he would fly it solo back to Michigan over the course of a few days.

He arrived at LAX and drove to the small airfield to meet his new Seawind 3000 for the first time. But once there, he discovered that the aircraft had not been flown in two years and was not in quite as good condition as he had been led to believe.

> The first problem was the brake cylinder on the pilot's side was not working. I learned that the owner put it in with the hoses reversed. So his hangar buddy came out to troubleshoot it and reverse the lines and bleed the lines. This occurred after starting it and attempting a taxi test. The owner had used my deposits to purchase new main tires and tubes, headsets, Dynon instrument display repair and updating, ADS-B and a GPS antenna.

He was dismayed to discover that the money he had sent to reserve the aircraft had been spent on making it airworthy. Worse, even after the work they had done, the Seawind was not in the condition described in the advertisement. In his statement, the pilot consistently refers to the seller as the owner of the aircraft, even though he had already purchased the plane.

> The owner mentioned that the hydraulic gauge doesn't work once in a while and to just tap it. He also said to just use the left aux. fuel pump; the one on the right had a button light not working.

The ex-owner of the Seawind did not seem to be the least bit bothered about its condition. When the pilot asked him why the aileron trim was not working, the owner said that it was coupled with the autopilot and would work when the autopilot was activated. A further issue with the elevator trim was similarly "brushed off" as being part of the autopilot.

> After a long day of commercial flying and review of the Seawind, including lunch at the airport of which he wanted me to pay for his lunch, which I did not. He paid and it was the worst burger. One bite was enough; he took me to a local hotel for the night.

The following day, the pilot discovered that the aircraft logs had been lost and the owner had recreated them "to the best of his abilities". He also discovered that the (previous) owner was not current and would not be able to act as Pilot in Command while the pilot learned the peculiarities of the Seawind; in fact, the owner refused to go up with the pilot at all. The pilot took the Seawind out for a flight on his own and found that the aircraft nose was pitching up for no apparent reason. He flew three circuits trying to troubleshoot the problem. Defeated, he decided to call it a day and land.

Unfortunately, he forgot to lower the landing gear.

As the aircraft came down onto the runway, there was a loud bang and the Seawind skidded along the runway. The pilot shut down the engine and, with the seller's assistance, raised the aircraft up on floor jacks until it was high enough that the pilot could extend the landing gear. They towed the aircraft off of the runway and to the parking area. The seller then took the pilot to buy a new inner tube for the right wheel, which had burst on the initial impact with the gear up. Then one of the seller's friends installed the new inner tube for the pilot.

The previous owner remained to answer a few more questions about the instrument display. When the pilot asked him about meeting at the airfield the next day, the seller told him that he wasn't available. The pilot was stunned. He was on his own with his new plane.

With a sinking feeling, the pilot decided that the best thing he could do was get out of California. Despite his inauspicious first flight, he took off at 15:00, intending to arrive at Taos, New Mexico after nightfall. He could spend the night there and then carry on.

He took off normally but as he levelled out, he found that the nose-up problem was getting worse. He had to use his knee, padded with a rag, to pin the controls and keep the aircraft in level flight. He kept this up for about 45 minutes before deciding that he needed to cut the flight short.

He contacted the tower at Four Corners Regional Airport, in Farmington, New Mexico, to say he was inbound to their airfield. The tower controller welcomed him and cleared the flight to land on runway 07. However, as the pilot entered the circuit to land, he found that "it quickly turned to night." As he passed the runway, he turned right for the base leg but found that he couldn't see the instruments or the runway.

> All lights were on and there was no landing light. I called the tower and informed them that I was in the dark. The Dynon [instrument display] also went dim and I had to use my phone light to activate the display to get brighter so I could read my speeds. Turning final, I had full pressure on the yoke to hold the nose down and I couldn't see the runway.

Now the runway side lights were on but, as he admits, it was his first night landing in over twenty years. In the US, night flying does not require a special rating but it can be very disorienting, especially at a new airfield in an aircraft that you've only just taken possession of. He continued his final descent and at about ten feet above the runway, he pulled back on the power.

The transition from flying to landing takes some finesse. First, the airspeed and rate of descent are decreased to make the transition as gentle as possible. As the aircraft approaches the ground, the pilot should carefully raise the nose, slowing the descent as the aircraft touches down.

However, instead of settling down onto the runway, the Seawind 3000 "ballooned up", floating above the runway with the nose up. This is a hard position to recover from, as the aircraft is now low and slow with no room to manoeuvre. For this reason, it is better to go around and set up for landing again.

But the pilot was worried about flying in the dark with his lights not working correctly. He decided that he would be better off getting the aircraft onto the ground.

Floating above the runway with no visual references, he stalled the aircraft; there was no longer enough lift to keep it flying. Effectively, it fell the remaining distance and landed hard slightly to the left of the runway.

He pushed the throttle in to steer the aircraft back onto the runway and taxied to the ramp. He was met there by what he describes as ground crew, most likely staff at the fixed-based operator who had gathered to get a better look. The crew helped him to secure the aircraft and get to a local hotel. He writes that he was shaking most of the night but eventually fell asleep.

The next morning, the pilot discovered that

he had damaged the tail in the hard landing. He powered up the aircraft but then when he attempted to taxi, he ran into a runway sign, which scraped the underside of the left wing and ripped the left wing flap.

Some of the staff from a fixed-based operator, a company providing aeronautical services for general aviation traffic, stopped work to watch and take photographs. One of them informed him that they'd notified the FAA who would very much like to speak to him.

He ended up on the phone speaking to a representative of the FAA who had heard some questionable things about his ability to be in command of his aircraft. The pilot explained at length about landing in the dark with a failed landing light and that yes, he had wiped out a couple of runway lights and a runway length sign, but he had also flown from Brackett Field to Farmington without any issues with airspace or endangering commercial traffic. The FAA man was, he said, satisfied with his explanation.

The fact is, the man had a valid pilot's licence, he'd renewed his medical two months before, and he had not done anything illegal. The FAA representative had no obvious grounds to do more than clarify what had happened and let the man know that his escapades were attracting notice.

The pilot found a certified aircraft repair hangar at the airfield and the mechanic there agreed to repair the aircraft, including looking into why the aircraft kept pitching up. They narrowed it down to the trim tab "servo", an aerodynamic lever which activates in response to the pilot moving the primary flight controls, adjusting the angle of the trim tab and holding it in the desired position.

> Riveting the flap and finding the trim tab servo on the tail elevator was pulled out from the servo. This caused the tremendous pressure to hold the nose down because it was stuck holding it up with the force of the wind. Upon further inspection found it was installed incorrectly from the construction of the aircraft. The threaded rod was only in 5/16" on one side of the clevis and an inch on the other. So the Mechanic was kind enough to take me to a hardware store and get a longer rod and put it into the servo correctly and test it.

The pilot remained in Farmington for three days while this and other issues were dealt with by the mechanic. Finally, he was ready to continue his flight. For the second leg, he planned to fly north along the western slope of the Rockies. He encountered some weather but was able to remain in VFR and continued north, following rivers and highways. He was much happier with the aircraft in flight but noted an issue with the left aileron.

> The left wing aileron trim tab servo was stuck slightly up. The previous owner said this trim only works with the autopilot on (well that is bull) so turning east after

a long two-hour flight up the western
slope, I had realized that the nose wanted
to pitch up again and it was getting worse.
Holding again the yoke forward with
my knee and a rag to help the pressure I
continued to O'Neal, NB.

He came in to land at O'Neill Municipal Airport
(KONL) in Holt County, Nebraska. As he crossed the
threshold, he again struggled with the flare. The
aircraft pitched up and floated rather than settling
on the runway. This time he applied full power to
keep the aircraft from stalling. He was more than
10 feet over the runway and to the left of it.

I managed to pitch nose down and
skipping crisscrossing the runway and
through the grass, I climbed to a safe
altitude. The airport manager called on
the radio and asked if I was OK. Then it
went quiet. I was on my own.

He went around and approached the runway
again, and again the Seawind ballooned up.

Upon getting to the runway the aircraft
lifted again without any input and this
time I applied pressure and bounced it
off the runway and over a couple runway
lights that got wrapped around the
landing gear.

He set up again for a third attempt and again
the aircraft ballooned up. The pilot could not
understand what was happening and never

seemed to consider this might be his landing technique, or lack of it. He went around again.

This time, he approached the runway at a higher speed and firm downward pressure on the yoke to keep the nose down. In his own words, he forced the aircraft to the ground. He ran off the runway and into the long grass, from where he taxied back onto the runway. The airport manager and his wife took a golf cart and went out to meet him and calm him down.

The airport manager confirmed that he'd watched the aircraft come in.

> I spent three days with this fellow. He landed gear up the day he bought [the aircraft] for 100+ grand in California. Then [he] ran off the runway in New Mexico, wiping out landing lights and the left flap. He repaired it, then we were his next stop. Five attempts to land, last one lost it on landing, creamed two runway lights.

He said that the weight and balance was "way aft, outside the envelope" which was why the pilot was struggling to land. Various issues were discovered with the aircraft, including that the servo trim motor, which had broken again, was not the correct motor for the trim.

The pilot ordered a new servo trim motor which was delivered to the airfield. He purchased some sand from a DIY store and filled a number of one gallon ziplock bags which he placed into the bow of the aircraft to weigh it down, a quick fix to shift the centre of gravity forward to help him keep the nose down on landing.

He installed the new servo himself and was pleased that it worked perfectly.

> The folks at and the airport were most helpful with tools and food. The last two nights I was able to sleep in the small terminal room that had a couple beds for tired pilots, also a lounge room. Getting up early each day to the sunrise and making coffee for the morning regulars who stop by and share stories.

Now that he'd finished the repairs, he prepared for the next leg of his flight to Michigan.

> The Manager and his wife were very busy and I didn't want to bother them anymore as I had made good friends with them as they were EAA builders and came from Virgin Galactic as engineers, and prior to that Blue Origin.

Of note: we are now halfway through the pilot's explanation submitted to the National Transport and Safety Board to explain why his Seawind 3000 ended up at the bottom of a lake.

He took off early that morning but then discovered that the new trim tab that he had installed was not working. The aircraft kept pitching up and he was struggling to keep it under control; he could not fly it to Michigan like this. He turned back and, in his words, forced the aircraft down. This time, he bounced hard to the left on touchdown, bending the left landing gear and scraping the brake cylinder.

Another pilot brought out the tug and helped to get the Seawind back into the hangar. He recommended that the pilot abandon the aircraft there in Nebraska and just take a commercial flight home. The pilot says that they told him that they would leave the aircraft as a display at the entrance of the airport.

I'm not sure that this was the compliment that he seemed to think it was.

The pilot had another look at the trim tab and found that he'd connected the grey wire on the wrong terminal, so the controls were reversed. He decided not to bother anyone for a second opinion and instead deal with it himself, despite the evidence that he was perhaps not the best person for this task.

He got a jack and tools from the airport manager and removed the brake and the bent aluminium leg from the landing gear. Then he used the courtesy car to try to find a metal shop. This was apparently no easy task and eventually, he writes, he found a John Deer dealer where he went in and they gave him directions to a metal shop which was just around the corner.

This is given considerably more detail than the actual repairs. Although I have never tried to repair an aircraft—maybe I am a bit overcautious—the quick fixes to the aircraft sound more and more worrisome as the saga continues. But the pilot was apparently happy (and still not interested in a second opinion).

The leg was straightened at the metal shop and the pilot put the plane back together again, presumably with the wires attached the right way 'round this time, and he slept in the terminal for one more night.

The pilot woke to bright sunshine the following morning and rewarmed some coffee before going out to the hanger. Although the airport manager and his wife lived on the airfield, the pilot decided he didn't want to wake them, so he attempted to push the Seawind out of the hanger on his own.

> Getting a few feet, I decided to just fire it up and get going. Taxied out to the runway and with full power lifted eastward into the morning sun. All things were normal. The takeoff, climb, and when getting into cruise at 7500 feet, the plane performed with finger touch control on the trims. Auto pilot was hands off, with a slight lift on the yoke to compensate for the non-working left aileron servo motor. The trim was slightly stuck in the up position.

The airport manager later told the story a bit differently, saying that the pilot was lucky to be alive. "It was like watching two trains heading towards one another...nothing you could do." He said that both he and his wife separately tried to convince him to ship the aircraft home to Michigan and take a commercial flight rather than fly it; however, he said that the pilot was "hellbent" on getting home. The FAA, after verifying that the pilot was qualified to fly, said to let him go.

According to the airport manager, the pilot sneaked out on Saturday without paying.

The pilot's version doesn't include any planning for the next leg of his trip home but he seemed to have been flying to Schoolcraft County Airport in Manistique, on the shores of Lake Michigan.

This flight was blissfully without incident until the pilot was almost at his destination, when he heard a loud clunk behind him. The left main gear, which he had straightened at the repair shop and reinstalled himself, had come down on its own. It wasn't registering any hydraulic pressure and he had no way to pull it back up. At the same time, he realised that the fuel gauge on the right side showed 5 gallons of fuel while he still had 35 gallons on the left side.

The fuel should have been automatically flowing between the two tanks in the aircraft wings to keep them equal but it wasn't happening. The centre of gravity, already shifted forward by the sandbags in the bow, was now heavily to the left, which was presumably what had caused the left landing gear to fall down.

As he was already close to the airport, he radioed ahead to say that he was inbound and asked if someone could help and see if the landing gear was down.

As he flew parallel to the runway, the right main landing gear came down on its own as well and he saw that he had two green lights. "Three greens" is a visual check that all three landing gears (left, right and nose) are down.

> Now just give me the nose. I cycled the
> gear switch but nothing happened. The
> gauge was at zero pressure. Turning left
> to base and, to my surprise, the engine
> sputtered as if to stop and after leveling
> out on base, it ran normal. Then on the
> turn to final it sputtered again, the fuel
> was flowing away from the boost pump.
> So leveling out on final, I had the engine
> running with less than four gallons of fuel
> and both main gear down and the nose
> gear still not down.

As he came down to the runway, he was pleased that the aircraft flared "without popping up". He landed on the main gears, keeping the nose up in the air for as long as he could. Once the nose came down, the aircraft skidded to a halt. He climbed out of the cockpit and took a look. He had suffered, he said, only minimal damage to the gear door and nose skin.

> So, looking back at the terminal about
> a half mile away, I hiked back over the
> brush and small lumps and ruts on this
> hot day. Getting there and seeing no one
> was there, but doors open for pilots. I
> went in and pondered what to do. My
> cell phone was turned off due to non-
> payment (maxed card).

He quickly reassures the National Transportation

and Safety Board that he had paid his phone bill, just that the payment hadn't gone through yet because of the holiday weekend.

A motel sat across the road, so he walked there and spoke to the new owners, a nice couple from Traverse City who let the pilot use their phone to call his son and then took him to a tractor supply store to buy a couple of quarts of hydraulic fluid.

> I thanked him for taking time out when he clearly didn't have time to do so. As I turned, the Michigan State Police with sirens and flashers came flying by, entered the airport, onto the runway and out to the crippled plane. Turning back, I thanked him again and said, "This is my cue, got to go." It was the excitement of the day for Manistique.

He returned to the terminal and sat on a picnic table until the police noticed him there and drove back. He confirmed that he was the only occupant of the aircraft and that he was OK, and that he'd only left to purchase some hydraulic oil to get the gear up (I'm pretty sure he meant down) and the aircraft off the runway.

They escorted him back to the aircraft where a police officer lifted the nose while the pilot pulled the gear down, after which he was able to taxi the aircraft to the terminal fuel-up area. The pilot shut down the engine and explained that he was now waiting for his son to arrive with his credit card so that they could refuel the plane, but it was about a three-hour drive.

He seemed surprised that the police officers phoned the FAA.

> Once again I was on the police phone talking to them explaining what had occurred.

He told the FAA representative that he was just flying home to Boyne City, a 25-minute flight from Manistique, and he agreed that he would leave the gear down so as to ensure a safe landing.

The pilot's son arrived with the pilot's grandchildren, as their mother was working.

> They really enjoyed sitting in the airplane and asking questions and seeing other small planes come in and park across from us. They had never been in an airplane before and wanted to go for a ride, which I quickly said was not a good idea, mom would not approve. And neither did I.

Well, thank goodness for small mercies.

When the pilot opened the right wing inboard tank, he was surprised to discover that it was full of fuel. The left inboard tank, which had shown as 35 gallons, however, was almost empty. He was at a loss: the gauge was showing the opposite of where the fuel was. The fuel pump was only needed for the outboard tip tanks. His next paragraph is just a list of questions as he wonders what might be wrong.

Some aircraft mix the fuel from the wings

automatically and some aircraft require the pilot to shift between the two tanks during flight to keep them balanced. The Seawind has a header tank which is automatically filled from the right and left tanks; only the wing tips, which hold additional fuel for long-range flights, require the pumps to transfer fuel into the main tanks.

The pilot didn't know that you can also pump the fuel from side to side if you have an issue like this, where the fuel isn't balanced between the wings. However, to do this, you rather need your gauges not to be reversed.

Somehow, after asking all these questions, the pilot decided that the correct course of action was to refuel the empty left tank and carry on to Boyne City, noting that he felt bad about his son having to drive with the kids all that way to rescue him.

The son and the grandchildren watched from the grass next to the terminal as the pilot departed for the last leg ("blasted off into the sky" is the description the pilot uses). He planned to climb to 7,500 feet to cross Lake Michigan, passing over Beaver Island, to Charlevoix on the opposite coast, after which he would turn right and follow the coast to Traverse City.

The aircraft climbed to 5,500 feet but then he found he was unable to keep climbing. The aircraft simply wouldn't gain any more altitude.

He continued across the lake. As he reached Beaver Island, the engine began to splutter. It seemed to recover but then spluttered again. By now he had passed the island and was over the water. The engine spluttered again and then stopped completely. He smelled something burning.

He turned back in hopes of landing on the island but quickly realised he wasn't going to make it.

> By then I was gliding down out of 5000 feet and I had to set it up for landing. Keep it at 90 MPH. I wanted flaps to help so I pressed the button and nothing. I looked at the hydraulic gauge and it was not registering any pressure at all. What was going on, I had just filled it. The pump must be out. So, no flaps. And the gear is down. This will be my first water landing.

It's not *really* a water landing with the landing gear down; in fact, I am going to have to agree with the NTSB that this is actually an attempted ditching in a sea plane, which in itself is an impressive feat.

His report on the accident becomes almost poetic.

> The sun was low on the horizon to my left and I could see the glitter of the sun on the water. Looking back at the panel and seeing my speed as steady and keeping the angle of descent I glanced back over the water and realized I could judge my altitude with the glittering of the sun over the small ripple of the water. Time seemed to slow and I was transfixed on the beauty of the sun over the water and keeping my eye on the water and the glide I could see

it coming and it was close, a few more
seconds and it was really close.

He adjusted the nose to flare, this time
hoping that the aircraft would stall and gently
fall onto the water's surface. Instead, the landing
gear struck the waves and the aircraft fell nose-
forward with a splash, descending beneath the
surface before popping back up. The pilot set
all of the switches to off and then opened the
canopy. He sat there in the sunlight, floating
gently, and waited for someone to find him.

But it might take some time.

He turned the switches back on and set his
transponder to squawk 7700, the international
code for aircraft in distress. He made a radio call
but received no response.

That's when he realised that the aircraft
was taking on water. He found a small plastic
container and started bailing the water out of
the aircraft. It soon became clear that he couldn't
keep up and the aircraft's tail was starting to sink.

He was going to have to abandon the plane.
He picked up his phone and his wallet and took
the seat back as a flotation device. He took his
shoes off. As the cockpit filled with water and the
left wing dipped under, he jumped onto the right
wing. He was soon waist deep in the water with
only the wing tip breaking the surface. As his
personal belongings floated out of the cockpit,
he imagined himself on the Titanic.

The Seawind continued to sink. Soon, the
cold water came up to his chest. He grabbed the
engine cowling and pulled himself up. The nose

dipped under the wave. He inched along the aircraft to the tail and pulled himself out of the water by grabbing the vertical stabiliser.

> The sun was setting and it was red and I saw no one around. Did they hear my call? I don't know. Resting and remaining as calm as I could, I thought of my kids, what we have been through in our lives. They are now married and [my son who bought the fuel] has a son and is father to two girls and a boy. My oldest son is expecting a girl in a few weeks. Will I ever see them again? What will they think of this, I thought. This stupid thing that I did. I'm at fault for believing I could fix this and get home. I just wanted to get home.
>
> Lifting my head and not wanting to see that I was still alone, I looked straight ahead and off the horizon, I could see a big US Coast Guard boat coming. I couldn't believe it; they were coming.

He dropped the seat back and grabbed the horizontal stabiliser to pull himself out of the water so that he could wave at the Coast Guard. It took them some time, he said, as he was 40 miles off of the coast of Charlevoix and several miles south of the Beaver Islands. He'd been in the water an hour.

View of pilot on sinking plane as taken from a US
Coastguard Helicopter

The Seawind 3000 was fitted with an
Emergency Locator Transmitter for exactly
this kind of emergency. When the unit was
submerged in water, it activated the distress
beacon, broadcasting his location on the
emergency frequencies. The Coast Guard had
immediately dispatched vessels from both sides
of the lake in order to find him.

He climbed up onto the last bit of the tail still
out of the water and the Coast Guard pulled him
on board. He says that as they turned the boat
around, the aircraft flipped over until only the
tip of the tail was sticking out.

If this feels a bit cinematic, that's not a
coincidence. He later told the local paper[18] that
he wrote out the first-person narrative while it
was fresh in his mind, "in case it had any motion

18   https://web.archive.org/web/20210725113707/
https://www.record-eagle.com/news/seawind-saga-pilot-
who-crashed-in-lake-michigan-had-7-crashes-in-7-days/
article_867676c0-e8d7-11eb-be82-db592d516d36.html

picture potential".

That same paper reports that the aircraft was not insured and that the whole experience was so traumatic, the pilot doesn't see himself piloting an airplane ever again.

I'm sure that all of the airport staff along his route gave a great sigh of relief on hearing that.

A representative from the U.S. Coast Guard stated that the amount of fuel in the aircraft was low enough that they were not concerned about it polluting the lake.

The NTSB report[19] notes that they did not travel to the scene of the crash.

The airplane was not recovered; therefore, the engine could not be examined, and the reason for the loss of engine power could not be determined. Additionally, based on the pilot's flight, it's likely the Seawind was not airworthy before the pilot's initial departure.

The FAA currently show multiple listings to do with this aircraft registration:

- June 26, 2021: Aircraft landed gear up at Brackett Field Airport (KPOC), La Verne, California.

- June 27, 2021: Aircraft veered off runway due to electrical issue and lost use of landing lights at Four Corners Regional Airport (KFMN), San Juan County, New Mexico.

- July 02, 2021: Aircraft landed hard and veered off runway at The O'Neill Municipal

19   https://data.ntsb.gov/carol-repgen/api/Aviation/ReportMain/GenerateNewestReport/103484/pdf

Airport (KONL), Holt County, Nebraska.

When asked for comment, the FAA would only say that they were investigating.

As a friend of mine said, "I don't feel too bad for him—the man actually did get the several decades of flying experience that he planned and paid for. He just crammed it all into one flight."

I hope that you enjoyed reading *Pilot Error* as much as I enjoyed creating it. But I'm not finished yet. Sign up to the Pilot Error mailing list at https://planecra.sh/error and you will be the first to know when the next book in the series is released. You'll also receive bonus material such as updates to the recent cases listed here.

Are you wondering what happened to the pilot who landed on the highway? Sign up to receive updates and bonus content!

If you enjoyed this book, I think you will also enjoy my series WITHOUT A TRACE, which tells the true stories of aircraft and passengers who disappeared into thin air; mysteries which have baffled investigators for years. Find out more at https://planecra.sh/without-a-trace.

About the Author

Sʏʟᴠɪᴀ Wʀɪɢʟᴇʏ is a pilot and aviation writer who has been obsessing about aviation safety for over a decade.

- Her non-fiction has appeared in publications all over the world, including *The Guardian, Piper Flyer* and *Forbes.*

- She has appeared as an aviation expert for the BBC and on *National Geographic's Mayday.* She has also featured in episodes of the Discovery Channel series *Air Crash Confidential,* the Russian Channel 1 news, French Channel M6 *Disparition du vol MH370* and ntv.ru *Central Television* program.

- She is the creator and sole contributor to the aviation website http://fearoflanding.com/ which received almost half a million visitors in 2019 and continues to be a leading aviation resource.

- **Aviation Books:**
  - *You Fly Like a Woman*
  - *Why Planes Crash Case Files: 2001*
  - *Why Planes Crash Case Files: 2002*
  - *Why Planes Crash Case Files: 2003*
  - *Without a Trace 1881–1968*
  - *Without a Trace 1970–2016*

Image Credits

Aircraft Parked at the Pub: Western Australia Police Force

That Airport Must Be Here Somewhere: Swiss Council for Accident Prevention BFU

How To Drop a Business Jet Into a Ravine: Massachusetts State Police

Mid-Air Collision on Approach: US National Transportation Safety Board

How Will We Stop the Engine, Then?: Rwanda Ministry of Infrastructure

Interfering With Helicopter Controls: Bell Textron Inc

Crop Duster Crashes in Gender Reveal Stunt: US National Transportation Safety Board

All Aircraft Bite Fools: US National Transportation Safety Board

Reckless River Flying: Australian Transport Safety Bureau

Fatal Seaplane Crash at Oshkosh: US National Tranportation Safety Board

On a Wing and a Prayer: US Coast Guard

References

All Boozed Up and Ready To Fly
https://www.airbaltic.com/en/airbaltic-introduces-additional-safety-measures
https://www.aftenposten.no/nyheter/iriks/Air-Baltic-styrmann-anker-promilledom-8138665.html
Highway Patrol Arrest Pilot
https://data.ntsb.gov/carol-repgen/api/Aviation/ReportMain/GenerateNewestReport/105515/pdf
https://www.kshb.com/news/local-news/witness-recalls-moments-leading-up-to-i-70-plane-landing-by-allegedly-intoxicated-pilot
N28V, I Need Your Call Sign, please
https://www.natca.org/community/awards/2018-archie-league-medal-of-safety-award-winners/
https://www.youtube.com/watch?v=7KGWM00p7Rg
Aircraft Parked at the Pub
https://www.9news.com.au/national/man-who-taxied-plane-to-pub-faces-charges/7067d98f-e7c5-41ab-ad75-d7e03d1e5e72
https://www.ndtv.com/offbeat/australian-man-fined-for-driving-plane-down-main-street-702585

That Airport Must Be Here Somewhere
https://www.sust.admin.ch/inhalte/AV-
berichte/1793_d.pdf
Um, Have You Landed?
https://data.ntsb.gov/carol-repgen/
api/Aviation/ReportMain/
GenerateNewestReport/88667/pdf
Giant 4241 Heavy, Confirm You Know Which
Airport You Are At
https://www.boeing.com/commercial/787/
https://www.wired.com/2013/11/
dreamlifter-wrong-airport/
Where Am I Again?
https://www.hertfordshiremercury.
co.uk/news/Uttlesford/Pilot-
fined-after-causing-havoc-over-
Stansted-airport-20130418102741.
htm?service=responsive
Ever Left the Parking Brake On?
https://www.gov.uk/aaib-reports/aaib-
investigation-to-emb-145ep-g-ckag
How to Drop a Business Jet Into a Ravine
https://www.ntsb.gov/investigations/
AccidentReports/Reports/AAR1503.
pdf
Mid-Air Collision on Approach
https://www.ntsb.gov/investigations/
Pages/CEN21FA215.aspx
How Will We Stop the Engine, Then?
https://web.archive.org/
web/20171031002456/https://
www.mininfra.gov.rw/fileadmin/
user_upload/aircraft/Final_Report_
of_CRJ_100.pdf

Activities Not Related To the Conduct of This Flight
https://data.ntsb.gov/carol-repgen/
api/Aviation/ReportMain/
GenerateNewestReport/32972/pdf
Interfering With Helicopter Controls
https://www.ntsb.gov/legal/alj/
OnODocuments/Aviation/5447.PDF
Jumping out of a Plane isn't Enough of a Thrill?
https://www.golfhotelwhiskey.com/
the-faa-investigates-a-sex-diving-
incident/
http://www.tinynibbles.com/
blogarchives/2011/10/skydiving-sex-
scandal-but-whos-getting-screwed.
html
Crop Duster Crashes in Gender Reveal Stunt
https://airtractor.com/aircraft/at-602/
https://data.ntsb.gov/carol-repgen/
api/Aviation/ReportMain/
GenerateNewestReport/100227/pdf
Impromptu Air Show
https://www.youtube.com/
watch?v=QwK9wu8Cxeo
https://www.youtube.com/
watch?v=VuDd6mjCl98
All Aircraft Bite Fools
https://data.ntsb.gov/carol-repgen/
api/Aviation/ReportMain/
GenerateNewestReport/89319/pdf
https://time.com/3693868/pilot-selfies-
airplane-crash/
Barrel Rolls for TikTok

https://www.tiktok.com/@lisa_herrera_
usa/video/7102651051345743150
Social Media Influencers Weigh Down Aircraft
https://data.ntsb.gov/carol-repgen/
api/Aviation/ReportMain/
GenerateNewestReport/97006/pdf
https://people.com/human-interest/pilot-
plane-crashed-instagram-influencers-
cocaine-system/
Vintage Plane Crash for YouTube
https://www.youtube.com/
watch?v=vbYszLNZxhM
https://s30121.pcdn.co/wp-content/
uploads/2022/04/Jacob-EOR-
2022WP010003-FOIA_Redacted.pdf
Reckless River Flying
https://www.atsb.gov.au/publications/
investigation_reports/2014/aair/ao-
2014-068
http://www.northernstar.com.au/
news/fresh-charge-over-air-
crash/2581233/
Fatal Seaplane Crash at Oshkosh
https://data.ntsb.gov/carol-repgen/
api/Aviation/ReportMain/
GenerateNewestReport/95685/pdf
https://fox11online.com/news/local/fox-
cities/eaa-seaplane-hit-wave-before-
it-went-down-in-lake-winnebago
How To Drown a Jet
https://data.ntsb.gov/carol-repgen/
api/Aviation/ReportMain/
GenerateNewestReport/61495/pdf
https://www.youtube.com/

watch?v=N1Yf6_MVTck
On a Wing and a Prayer
https://data.ntsb.gov/carol-repgen/
api/Aviation/ReportMain/
GenerateNewestReport/103484/pdf

http://www.kathrynsreport.com/2021/07/
seawind-3000-n8uu-july-02-2021-
june-26. html?showComment=16257
22450373#c5273196280675555639
html?showComment=162572245037
3#c5273196280675555639

Printed in Great Britain
by Amazon

42434798R00145